"Come to me,
all you who labor and are burdened,
and I will give you rest."

JESUS OF NAZARETH

Matthew 11:28

"Whoever is in Christ is a new creation."

PAUL THE APOSTLE

2 Corinthians 5:17

"Ask and you will receive,
seek and you will find;
knock and the door will be opened to you."

JESUS OF NAZARETH

Luke 11:9

BEACON

Rediscover Jesus

AN INVITATION

MATTHEW KELLY

Rediscover Jesus

Hardcover ISBN-978-1-942611-19-6
Paperback ISBN-978-1-942611-20-2
Audiobook ISBN-978-1-942611-38-7
Ebook ISBN-978-1-942611-39-4

Designed by Leah Nienas

The Dynamic Catholic Institute
5081 Olympic Blvd • Erlanger, Kentucky 41018
Phone: 1–859–980–7900
Email: info@DynamicCatholic.com

For more information visit:
www.DynamicCatholic.com

First Edition

[2]

Printed in the United States of America

Table of Contents

PROLOGUE

Are you Jesus?

OUR GOD IS A GOD OF SURPRISES.

It was the biggest meeting of Paul's life, and it had gone well. He couldn't wait to tell his wife and his boss. As he rushed out of the Brooklyn office building with the rest of the team, they noticed a vacant cab—a rare sight during rush hour.

Eager to get to the airport to catch their flight home, they bolted toward the cab, yelling to get the driver's attention. But as they made their way across the sidewalk, they inadvertently knocked over a small produce stand. The rest of the team seemed oblivious until Paul stopped and turned around to go back.

From beside the taxi the others called out to Paul, "Come on, you'll miss your flight."

"Go ahead without me," Paul replied as he made his way back across the street toward the sidewalk covered in produce. At that moment, he realized that the woman who had been behind the produce stand was blind. She was just standing there crying softly with tears running down her face.

"It's OK, it's OK," Paul said to her as he got down on his hands and knees and began picking up the fruit and vegetables. There were a hundred people passing in each direction, but nobody else stopped to help. They just scurried off to wherever they were going.

When the fruit was all back up on the stand, Paul began neatly organizing it, setting aside anything that was spoiled. Now he turned to the woman and asked, "Are you OK?" She nodded through her tears. Then, reaching for his wallet, he took out some bills and passed them to the woman, saying, "This money should cover the damages."

With that, Paul turned and began to walk away.

"Mister," the woman called after him. Paul paused and turned around. "Are you Jesus?"

"Oh, no," he replied.

The woman nodded and continued, "I only ask because I prayed for Jesus to help me as I heard my fruit falling all over the sidewalk."

Paul turned to leave again, only now his eyes began to fill with tears.

For a long time he wandered around looking for a taxi. After finally finding one, he sat in bumper-to-bumper traffic all the way to the airport. He had missed his flight, and because it was Friday night, all the other flights were full.

Paul spent the night in a hotel by the airport. This gave him time to think. He couldn't get one question out of his head: When was the last time someone confused you for Jesus?

POINT TO PONDER: Jesus wants you to carry on his work.

VERSE TO LIVE: "Seek first the kingdom of God and his righteousness." MATTHEW 6:33

QUESTION TO CONSIDER: How much is the sheer busyness of your life preventing you from living the life God is calling you to live?

PRAYER: Jesus, give me the courage to let down my guard.

Opening Thoughts

THE BEST TIME TO REDISCOVER Jesus is right now.

You are holding this book in your hand at this very moment for a reason. I don't know what God has in store for you, but I am excited for you.

There are some questions that we all ask ourselves in different ways: Who am I? Who is God? What am I here for? What matters most? What matters least? What are my unique talents and abilities? What will my contribution be? What happens when we die?

We are constantly grappling with these questions. Jesus is the amazing friend who is going to help you answer them. Jesus is the amazing friend who is going to help you live the answers once you find them. Jesus is the amazing friend who is going to be at your side through it all.

If you don't already have this kind of relationship with Jesus, I only ask that you stay open to the possibility. He wants to have a dynamic relationship with you.

There are two ways to experience this book. The first is like with any other book: Read it from cover to cover. The other way is to use this book as a guide to a forty-day spiritual journey, reading a chapter a day. This second way is a perfect way to begin (or nourish) a habit of daily prayer.

At the end of each chapter you will find a Point to Ponder, a Verse to Live, a Question to Consider, and a short Prayer. These are designed to help you integrate what you learn in each chapter into your life.

But this book is not about the words on the page. It's about an encounter. My deep longing is that it facilitates a powerful encounter between you and Jesus, because whether we are aware of it or not, what you and I need more than anything else is to encounter Jesus. Whatever is happening in your life right now, nothing is more important than encountering him anew.

Some books find us at just the right time in our lives, and those books change our lives forever. I hope this is that kind of book for you.

ONE

New Beginnings

GOD LOVES NEW BEGINNINGS.

Do you ever feel like you need a new beginning? That's exactly how I was feeling not too long ago. I was tired and frustrated, a little disoriented spiritually, disgusted with some of the things happening in the world and in the Church, and distracted by so many situations that I could do absolutely nothing about.

I probably needed to recite the Serenity Prayer about a thousand times.

God, Grant me the serenity
to accept the things I cannot change;
courage to change the things I can;
and wisdom to know the difference.

But I didn't have the presence of mind to do even that.

At first I just ignored all these feelings and tried to keep busy. But ignoring things doesn't make them go away. It took a while, but finally I realized that I needed a new beginning.

One of the things I love about our faith is that our God is a God of second chances, fresh starts, and new beginnings.

I love Mondays, because each Monday is a new beginning—a fresh start! God gives us Mondays, and New Year's Day, and birthdays, and every single one represents a new blessing and a new beginning.

In the Bible we read these epic tales of the incredible ways that God transformed people and their lives: Moses, Noah, Jonah, Jeremiah, David, Joseph, Mary, Peter, James, Matthew, Zacchaeus, Paul, Lydia, Mary Magdalene, the woman at the well, and so many others whose names we don't know. Why not you and me? Why not now?

God is always waiting on us. Sometimes we may think we are waiting for him, but that is never true.

What's happening in your life right now? What's not working in your life? What great question are you grappling with in your heart? Why did you pick up this book? Do you need a fresh start too?

Whenever I get to a place in my life where things aren't making sense, it always seems that I need to rediscover Jesus.

Jesus is the ultimate new beginning.

POINT TO PONDER: It is never too late for a fresh start.

VERSE TO LIVE: "Ask and it will be given to you; search and you will find; knock, and the door will be opened for you."
MATTHEW 7:7

QUESTION TO CONSIDER: In what area of your life is God inviting you to experience a new beginning?

PRAYER: Jesus, help me to believe that a new beginning is possible.

TWO

Getting to Know Jesus

GOD THE FATHER WANTS US to know his Son.

How well do you know Jesus? I think about this often, and I always come to the same realization: I don't know Jesus anywhere near as well as I would like to know him. The desire is there, but life gets in the way. There are times when I seem to be making great progress, and other times when I wonder if I know him at all.

But I always arrive back at the same inspiring and haunting idea: If there is one person we should each get to know in a deeply personal way, it is Jesus—the carpenter from Nazareth, the itinerant preacher, the Son of God, the King of Kings and the Lord of Lords, the Lamb of God, the new Adam, the Messiah, the alpha and the omega, the chosen one, the light of the world, the Godman who wants good things for us more than we want them for ourselves, the healer of our souls.

How well do you know him? Give yourself a score right now between one and ten. Sure, it's a hard thing to measure, but you know if you're a two or an eight. You might not know if you are a 6.453, but you have a sense of where you are on the spectrum.

Think about all the people in your life. You have your immediate and extended family and your closest friends. Then there are the people you spend a lot of time with simply because your lives overlap—not necessarily by choice, but as a result of work, school, or your children's schedules. You also have acquaintances—people you know just a little bit, whom by chance or choice you have never really gotten to know. And of course, there are people who just cross your path—strangers.

Where does Jesus fit into the spectrum of people in your life?

I don't know Jesus anywhere near as well as I should, and my relationship with him isn't nearly as dynamic as I would like it to be. And the thing that unsettles me is that sometimes I think I know people on the periphery of my life better than I know Jesus.

Try this: Grab some paper and write down everything you know about Jesus. Everything. You may be surprised how quickly you run out of things to write. I was.

Consider this: How would you describe Jesus to someone who knows nothing about him? You'd probably tell the story—but how well do you know the story of Jesus Christ? It is the most powerful story ever told. But it loses its power when we take it for granted. It loses its power when we become so familiar with it that we stop hearing it as part of our own story. When we remove ourselves from the story of Jesus Christ we become immune to the life-changing message of the Gospel and become slaves to the world.

It's time to rediscover Jesus.

Have you ever met someone and discovered he was nothing like what you thought he would be? Before you met him, you knew about him. But knowing *about* someone is not the same as *knowing* someone.

Whenever I make the effort to rediscover Jesus, he surprises me. He confounds the stereotypes, reveals unconsidered possibilities, rearranges my priorities, liberates me from the chaos of the world, reminds me what matters most and what matters least, and brings real order to my life.

Jesus fills me with the lightheartedness that comes from knowing that our Father in heaven does indeed have a plan—even when I am too blind to see it, too arrogant to trust it, or too foolish to surrender to it.

Yes, I think it's time for me to rediscover Jesus, and I'd like to invite you to join me.

Who is Jesus? He's an invitation. There are so many ways to answer that question, but in a very simple and beautiful way Jesus is God's invitation to live an incredibly abundant and fulfilling life.

POINT TO PONDER: Jesus wants to have a deep, dynamic, personal relationship with you.

VERSE TO LIVE: "I am the Good Shepherd." JOHN 10:11

QUESTION TO CONSIDER: How well do you really know Jesus?

PRAYER: Jesus, open my heart and my mind so that I can get to know you as you really are.

Note: Throughout this book the word Gospel *is used in different ways. It is used in general to refer to the teachings of Jesus. On occasion it is used more specifically to refer to one of the first four books of the New Testament—Matthew, Mark, Luke, and John. When the plural,* Gospels, *is used, this always refers to the first four books of the New Testament.*

THREE

An Invitation

A GOOD INVITATION FILLS US WITH JOY.

More books have been written about Jesus than about any other person or subject in history. This book you are holding is not a book with all the answers. It is just a simple, approachable, digestible starting point for anyone who shares my yearning to rediscover Jesus. It too is an invitation.

There is a wonderful joy that comes from discovering something (or someone) for the first time. There is also an immense joy that comes from *re*discovering something (or someone). When I come home from a trip, whether I have been gone for two days or two weeks, I get the joy of rediscovering my wife and children.

To rediscover is a beautiful thing. It's time to rediscover Jesus—not just for our own sake, but for our children and their children, for the sake of our local church communities, for society at large, and for all humanity.

Look around you. The world is constantly grappling with crisis and war. People are weary from the dysfunction of their own lives. The chaos is crying out for order. The complexity is crying out for simplicity. At every level in society, from the beggar on the street to the leaders of nations, we are all looking for *something* to solve the crisis of our lives and of our times.

It is time to stop looking for some*thing* and start looking to some*one*—Jesus of Nazareth. For more than two thousand years he has been performing miracles in the lives of ordinary men and women. Now he wants to perform miracles in you and through you.

Are you ready?

POINT TO PONDER: It's time to stop everything, pause a little, and consider God's invitation.

VERSE TO LIVE: "I came so that they may have life and have it more abundantly." JOHN 10:10

QUESTION TO CONSIDER : What area of your life will benefit most from accepting God's invitation to rediscover Jesus?

PRAYER: Jesus, thank you for all the times you have invited me to rediscover you and your message. Help me not to squander this opportunity.

FOUR

The Jesus Question

LIFE IS FULL OF QUESTIONS.

Some are large and others are small. Some are essential and others are trivial. Some of life's questions are passing curiosities that we ponder once and never return to, but others provide the themes of our lives. These enduring questions are at the core of everything that happens in us and around us. In many ways, the questions we ask of ourselves, of others, and of society define who we become.

There is one question that we all have to answer eventually. I call it the Jesus question. Some people go looking for it, chasing it with the joyful abandon of a child in a treasure hunt. Others spend their whole lives avoiding the question. Some people try to tiptoe quietly toward it, while others stomp up to it, lacking even an ounce of the humility and reverence required to sit thoughtfully with it. For some people the question unexpectedly jumps out at them one day in the midst of their daily affairs. Some people discover the question through the once-in-a-lifetime friendship of someone who introduces them to the Jesus they have always known about but never really known. For others a tragedy drops the question on the doorstep of their lives.

Sometimes we fill our lives with noise and busyness to avoid the Jesus question, but when the noise finally dies down and the busyness subsides, the question is still there. It waits patiently to be pondered and answered.

There are some people who quote somebody else's answer to the question, but someone else's answer is profoundly insufficient. We each need our own answer to the Jesus question. It is a deeply personal question that requires a deeply personal answer.

I suspect that how we deal with this particular question says much about who we are and what we value. I'm sure it has to do with nature and nurture. Then there are the biases, prejudices, and blind spots we carry with us as a result of a lifetime of past experiences. And, of course, there are the fears and ambitions that we so often allow to rule our lives. But this type of analysis can also become a way of avoiding the question itself.

The question itself is like Jesus. Agree with him or disagree with him. Glorify him or vilify him. Follow him or reject him. About the only thing you cannot do when it comes to Jesus is ignore him. He is inescapable and unavoidable. His fingerprints are everywhere. He changed the world—in some ways that most people are aware of, and in countless ways that the average person has simply never considered.

Try as you might, you cannot escape him. Jesus is the inescapable friend who only ever wants your highest good. Everything that is good and desirable he wants for you even more than you want these good things for yourself. It doesn't matter how rude you are to him; he will wait patiently, until you surrender to the wisdom required to delve deep into the Jesus question.

The Jesus question is here to stay, not just for Christians, but for all men and all women of goodwill—and even men and women of ill will. You can try to ignore it, or dodge it, or dismiss it, but in the end, everybody has to answer the Jesus question.

•••••

If we were discussing these things over coffee, by now you would probably want to interrupt and ask, "OK, so what is the Jesus question?"

Several years ago I was in Israel with a group of pilgrims, walking where Jesus walked. On the second day of our trip we found ourselves at the ruins in Caesarea Philippi. Our guide's name was Nedal. He was learned and wise. He knew the region and history, but you could also tell that for him it was personal. His teaching on that day entranced me. He brought the following story from Matthew's Gospel to life, and I have been pondering it in new ways ever since.

Jesus was walking with his disciples in the district of Caesarea Philippi when he asked them two questions. The first question was: "Who do people say that I am?" The disciples replied, "Some say John the Baptist, others Elijah, still others Jeremiah or one of the prophets" (Matthew 16:13–20).

The second question Jesus asked was: "But who do you say that I am?"

This is the Jesus question. Who do *you* say that Jesus is? Not who do your parents or teachers, spouse, pastor, or friends say that Jesus is, but who do you say he is? This is the inescapable question about the unavoidable Jesus. Sooner or later, we each have to proclaim for ourselves who we think Jesus is.

As I read this passage and imagine the disciples gathering around Jesus as he asks these questions, I get the sense that the disciples were a little hesitant. Perhaps they were looking around at each other wondering if these were trick questions. They were richly human and so I imagine them playfully saying, "You take this one, Peter!"

There were many aspects to Peter, as there are to us all. But the leader in Peter recognized the importance of that moment, and he stepped up and said, "You are the Messiah, the Son of the living God!"

If Jesus showed up to your church this Sunday and stood before everyone and said, "Who do people say that I am today?" what would we tell him?

Our culture seems intent on placing Jesus in the same category as Santa Claus and the Easter Bunny. But Jesus is not a figment of Christian imagination. He lived in a place and a time; he walked the earth as you and I do today. The historical evidence of Jesus is irrefutable. Christian records and writings are more comprehensive than any other ancient texts. Jewish historians clearly established Jesus in history, and the major secular historian of his time also acknowledged him.

There is also a growing number of people who want to reduce Jesus to just a nice guy. Not *the* nice guy, or even the *nicest* guy, but just one of many nice guys. As a result of this type of thinking, there are many people who want to reduce the essence of Christianity to simply being a nice person.

Countless people and cultures since the time of Jesus have come up with countless ways to diminish who he was and what that means to humanity, history, and each of us individually. Our own time is not unique or different in this way.

The world's other major religions believe that Jesus was either a great teacher or a great prophet. It is first interesting and important to note that they do not deny his existence or the fact that he lived and walked the earth at a certain time in a particular place.

But Jesus did not claim to be a great teacher or a great prophet. Who did Jesus claim to be?

_____

POINT TO PONDER: Right now you have an incredible opportunity to get to know Jesus better.

VERSE TO LIVE: "I came into the world to testify to the truth. Everyone who belongs to the truth listens to my voice." JOHN 18:38

QUESTION TO CONSIDER: Have you ever really explored the Jesus question?

PRAYER: Jesus, teach me to never stop seeking you. Help me to seek you in every relationship, place, and situation.

_____

FIVE
The God Claim

THE EVIDENCE IS OVERWHELMING AND INSPIRING.

More than any other person in history, Jesus had clarity about his identity. He was clear about who he was and who he wasn't. Some wanted him to be a political leader or military revolutionary, but he refused. Others wanted him to be an economic savior, but he refused. Many tried to use him for their own personal gain, but he constantly evaded them.

So, perhaps it's worth exploring who Jesus thought he was by asking: What did Jesus say about himself?

Directly and indirectly throughout the Gospels, Jesus said he was God. In the Gospels he referred to himself as the "Son of Man" eighty times. It was his favorite name. What does it mean? What is the significance? The prophet Daniel wrote: "As the visions during the night continued, I saw one like a son of man coming on the clouds of heaven; when he reached the Ancient One and was presented before him, he received dominion, glory, and kingship; nations and people of every language serve him. His dominion is an everlasting dominion that shall not be taken away, his kingship shall not be destroyed" (Daniel 7:13–14).

So, when Jesus said, "I am the Son of Man," he was saying:

I am the one Daniel spoke about. I have dominion, glory, and kingship. . . . Every nation will worship me. . . . People of every language will serve me. . . . My dominion is divine. Worldly dominion can be taken away, but my dominion is not worldly and it cannot be taken from me. . . . My kingship is divine. The kings of this world can be murdered and overthrown, their kingship and kingdoms can be destroyed, but my kingship is inseparable from who I am. It cannot be taken or transferred to anybody else. . . . I am the one you have been waiting for.

When you and I read the passage today, much of the meaning may be lost on us, but it was not lost on the Jewish people of Jesus' time—or their religious leaders. They were not confused about what Jesus was claiming. That's why they accused him of blasphemy. That's why they tried to stone him to death, because that was the punishment for blasphemy. Jesus claimed to be God.

When Jesus said, "I am the Son of Man," he was speaking their language. They knew exactly what he was saying. He was saying to them, "I am the Messiah. I am the rightful heir to the divine throne. Nations will worship me and I will rule forever. My kingdom is untouchable and unstoppable. I am the fulfillment of Daniel's vision."

This is what Jesus had to say about himself. Over and over throughout the Gospels he demonstrated his divinity with both his words and actions. He indirectly asserted his divinity in dozens of ways to help the people of his time connect the dots between what he was doing and saying and what the prophets had been saying about the long-awaited Messiah for thousands of years.

Jesus demonstrated control over nature.

"Then he got up, rebuked the winds and the sea, and there was great calm. What sort of man is this, whom even the winds and the sea obey?" (Matthew 8:26–27).

When Jesus demonstrated his control over nature, it clearly signified his divinity. But we also see that even during his lifetime people were grappling with the Jesus question when they asked: "What sort of man is this?"

Jesus claimed he was able to forgive sins.

"He entered a boat, made the crossing, and came into his own town. And there people brought him a paralytic lying on a stretcher. When Jesus saw their faith, he said to the paralytic, "Courage, child, your sins are forgiven."

Jesus brings order to everything. The people were focused on the paralytic's physical needs, but Jesus essentially said, "You need forgiveness more than you need physical healing."

At that some of the scribes said to themselves, "This man is blaspheming." Jesus knew what they were thinking, and said, "Why do you harbor evil thoughts? Which is easier, to say, 'Your sins are forgiven,' or to say, 'Rise and walk'? But that you may know that the Son of Man has authority on earth to forgive sins"—he then said to the paralytic, "Rise, pick up your stretcher and go home." When the crowds saw this they were struck with awe . . ." (Matthew 9:1–7)

Only God can forgive sins. By claiming authority to forgive sins, Jesus was again claiming to be God. In this situation he backed up his claim by making the lame walk.

Notice the reaction of the people. They were awestruck. When is the last time you were awestruck by Jesus? Why is it that we won't allow ourselves to be awestruck by Jesus anymore? Have our hearts become too hardened? Have we become too cynical? Have we become so familiar with the astounding acts of Jesus' life that we are no longer impressed?

Jesus claimed to be the Lord of the Sabbath.

"The Sabbath is made for man, not man for the Sabbath. That is why the Son of Man is lord even of the Sabbath" (Mark 2:27–28).

In modern times we may read this and miss most of the meaning, but the Sabbath was at the center of Jewish life and customs. It was sacred. Don't forget, keeping the Sabbath is the third commandment. Who is the author of the Ten Commandments? God. God is lord of the Sabbath. So by claiming authority over what was and was not permitted on the Sabbath, Jesus was claiming to be God.

Jesus demonstrated he had power over death.

When Jesus arrived, he found that Lazarus had already been in the tomb for four days. . . . When Martha heard that Jesus was coming, she went to meet him. . . . Martha said to Jesus, "Lord, if you had been here my brother would not have died. But even now I know that whatever you ask of God, God will give you." Jesus said to her, "Your brother will rise." Martha said to him, "I know he will rise, in the resurrection on the last day. Jesus said, "I am the resurrection and the life, whoever believes in me, even if he dies, will live, and everyone who lives and believes in me will never die. Then Jesus approached the tomb and said, "Lazarus, come out!" and the dead man came out of the tomb. (John 11: 1–44)

Notice that Martha believed that Jesus had the power to prevent the death of her brother.

When was the last time you were at a funeral? Imagine the scene if someone had walked in, opened the coffin, and said to the dead person, "Come out!" and that dead person had gotten up and walked out. Imagine. There would be complete pandemonium.

Jesus wants your funeral to be a resurrection too.

Power over death belongs to God. By demonstrating that he had power over death, Jesus was displaying his divinity. This was powerfully demonstrated when he raised Lazarus from the dead. Raising Lazarus was also a dramatic foreshadowing of the central event upon which all of Christianity hinges: the Resurrection.

POINT TO PONDER: Jesus is speaking directly to you in the Gospels.

VERSE TO LIVE: "I am the Way, and the Truth, and the Life." JOHN 14:6

QUESTION TO CONSIDER: What's holding you back from believing in Jesus completely?

PRAYER: Lord Jesus, I trust in you.

SIX

There Is More

THERE IS SO MUCH MORE.

There is more to God than we can imagine or discover in this life. There is more to life than most of us realize for most of our lives. And there is so much more to Jesus than can be contained in this short book, which is why I will say it again: This book is just the beginning of a journey that I hope will last the rest of your life.

Now let's explore some more of Jesus' claims about himself.

Jesus claimed to be able to give eternal life.

"My sheep hear my voice; I know them, and they follow me. I give them eternal life, and they shall never perish" (John 10:27–28).

Jesus showed people how to have a richer, deeper, more meaningful life here on earth. But he also reminded them that there is more to the human experience than this life. He pointed them to the eternal. Many people have done this throughout history.

Many wise leaders and teachers have helped people to have a deeper experience of life and pointed them toward the eternal. But Jesus went a step further. He claimed to be able to *give* people everlasting life.

Jesus claimed to be the Messiah.

"Again the high priest asked him and said to him, 'Are you the Messiah, the son of the Blessed One?' Then Jesus answered, 'I am'" (Mark 14:61–62).

Who did Jesus say he was? When we explore this question there is no confusion. Over and over again, throughout his public life Jesus made it clear that he was the long-awaited Messiah spoken of throughout the Old Testament. He made it clear that he was God.

Jesus claimed he could see into the future.

"Then he took the twelve aside and said to them, 'Behold, we are going up to Jerusalem and everything written by the prophets about the Son of Man will be fulfilled. He will be handed over to the Gentiles and he will be mocked and insulted and spat upon; and after they have scourged him they will kill him, but on the third day he will rise'" (Luke 18:31–33).

A great mind can study all of history's yesterdays, but only God can see into the future and foretell every tomorrow. Jesus often told his disciples about future events. His knowledge of the future was a display of his divinity.

Jesus claimed to preexist the world.

"Now glorify me, Father, with you, with the glory that I had with you before the world began" (John 17:5).

Who created the world? God did. So, when Jesus claimed to have existed before the world began, he was again claiming to be God. Once we really begin to consider the claims of Jesus, the Gospel becomes a litany of stories that announce, "Jesus is God!"

But for anyone who was unclear about what he was claiming, Jesus removed all doubt when he said, "The Father and I are one"(John 10:30) and "Whoever has seen me has seen the Father" (John 14:9).

•●◆●•

When you take all this into account it is easy to see how the early Christians came to the conclusion that Jesus was divine. Jesus said that he was God, and presented plenty of evidence to support his claim. The next generation of Christians believed based on the powerful testimony of those who had known Jesus, walked with him, listened to him teach, and witnessed his incredible actions. This testimony has been handed down from one generation to the next, at first orally, then in the form of handwritten manuscripts, and today in the Gospels you find in your Bible.

And perhaps the most powerful and compelling testimony is that eleven of the twelve disciples (all except John) died rather than deny what they knew to be true about Jesus' life, death, and resurrection.

Still each of us must answer the Jesus question for ourselves.

But let's be very clear about something. If Jesus is not who he claimed to be, he is a liar, but not just your average liar—he's the biggest liar in the history of the world. And if Jesus is not who he claimed to be, then he perpetrated the biggest fraud in history and every church you drive past is a monument to that fraud.

Is it really possible? What kind of conspiracy theory would be required to turn Jesus into the biggest liar and fraudster in the history of the world?

C. S. Lewis was one of the clearest thinkers of the twentieth century. In his book *Mere Christianity*, he indirectly addressed the Jesus question when he wrote:

> A man who was merely a man and said the sort of things Jesus said would not be a great moral teacher. He would either be a lunatic—on the level with a man who says he is a poached egg—or he would be the devil of hell. You must take your choice. Either this was, and is, the Son of God, or else a madman or something worse. You can shut him up for a fool or you can fall at his feet and call him Lord and God. But let us not come with any patronizing nonsense about his being a great human teacher. He has not left that open to us.

There is no evidence that Jesus was a lunatic. If he had been, his enemies would have been able to easily discredit him and shut him up. There would have been no need for a crucifixion if he were merely a lunatic.

For those who delve into the question with a humble heart, the evidence is overwhelming, and sooner or later they each arrive at the same conclusion: Jesus is who he claimed to be.

But answering the Jesus question is not easy. Is he a liar, a lunatic, or God? Each of us must arrive at our own answer, in our own time. What other people say can help us gain insight, but ultimately we must arrive at that answer on our own.

The Jesus question is not one to be taken lightly. So much is at stake—more than we can possibly imagine. But I suppose ultimately it comes down to deciding whether or not you believe Jesus.

POINT TO PONDER: Knowing *about* Jesus is not the same as *knowing* Jesus.

VERSE TO LIVE: "Do not be conformed to this world, but be transformed by the renewing of your minds, so that you may discern what is the will of God—what is good and acceptable and perfect." ROMANS 12:2

QUESTION TO CONSIDER: Do you have a really good reason not to take Jesus at his word?

PRAYER: Jesus, I believe. Help me to grow out of my doubts and unbelief.

SEVEN
The Third Question

GOD'S OPINION MATTERS THE MOST.

In Caesarea Philippi that day, Jesus asked his followers, "Who do people say that I am?" and "Who do you say that I am?" But there is a third question that doesn't appear in the sacred texts of the Gospel; nonetheless it is worthy of our consideration. It is a question that may also help us to understand and answer the Jesus question.

The third question is this: Who does Jesus say that you are?

Jesus says you are a child of God.

There are few things more precious in this world than the love of a mindful father. Selfishness and human weakness rob so many people of this experience, but when we see the beauty of true fatherhood it is unmistakably attractive.

A good father takes care of his children. He does everything he can to give his children what they need to live, learn, grow, and thrive. He doesn't give them everything they ask for. He weighs each request. And sometimes he gives them things they don't need, even before they ask, just to see them filled with joy. A good father always wants what is best for his child, and he sacrifices in a thousand ways for the sake of his child.

Jesus says you are a child of God. He came to remind us of the love God the Father has for each and every one of us.

The image of God that Jesus encouraged us to cling to was that of God as our Father (see Matthew 6:9).

I have always believed that God loves me. I'm not sure how or why. Perhaps it is because I always knew that my own father loved me. He wanted what was best for me. I never doubted that. We disagreed at times, but never once did I think he was acting out of selfishness. He cared for me, protected me, and made incredible sacrifices so that I could have opportunities he never had. He comforted me in my failures and rejoiced with me in my successes. More than anything, my father delighted in just being with me.

There was a time when I pretended I didn't believe in God. My grandmother had died and we were at her house after the funeral. I was sitting on the stairs of the front porch and my dad came out and sat down next to me. I said to him in an angry, tear-strained voice, "I don't believe in God anymore!" My dad didn't overreact. He responded calmly, "That's OK. God still believes in you."

Many years later, being a father myself has changed me in so many ways, and taken my spirituality to a whole new level. When I put my children to bed at night, we have a routine made up of various rituals unique to each child. Walter and I talk about his day, watch one of the many videos I have of my children on my phone, then I tell him a story, and finally we have prayer time. Isabel and I talk about her day, have story time and prayer time, and then we have a slow dance while I sing to her. Harry howls with laughter when I slap the book shut at the end of the story, but then he wants to read the same book again, and again. Finally, he says good night to Jesus and gives the picture of Jesus in his room a big, sloppy kiss. Every night I tell them, "No matter what happens, Daddy always loves you. And if you ever have a problem, you just come to Daddy and Daddy will help you fix it."

The love I have for my own children has proven to me beyond doubt that God loves me. Where does this love that I have for my children come from? Nothing comes from nothing. You see, if I can love my children the way I do—and I am wounded, imperfect, and broken—imagine how much God the Father loves us.

Yes, there are some horrible fathers in this world. But there are also some amazing fathers, and we know a great father when we see one. Think of the best father you know. Now multiply everything good about that father by infinity and you will still have barely a glimpse of God the Father.

Who does Jesus say you are? He says you are a child of God.

Jesus says you are infinitely valuable.

Jesus believes that you are infinitely valuable. Anytime you don't believe that, you are living in a state of deception, disconnected from the deepest, truest reality.

I often wonder how we would live our lives differently if we really understood our true value. Over and over, throughout the Scriptures, Jesus tries to affirm our value: "You are the light of the world" (Matthew 5:14). "You are the salt of the earth" (Matthew 5:13). You are my brothers and sisters (Matthew 12:50). You are so valuable that God has counted and keeps track of every hair on your head (Luke 12:7).

So often the world wants to belittle us and put us down. The world can be so impersonal, reducing us to numbers or defining us by our functions. But Jesus offers a radically different view.

He says you are infinitely valuable. In great contrast to the depersonalization of the world, Jesus affirms God's personal interest in you, even to the numbering of the hairs on your head. Jesus wants to raise you up. And more than anything else, he affirms that your value is not derived from what you do, but from who you are—a child of God.

Jesus says you are free.

Jesus values freedom above all else. God values freedom so much that he gives you the freedom to reject him. Without freedom there is no love, because we can only ever love to the extent that we are free.

The world treats us like orphans and slaves, but Jesus reminds us that we are children of God and that he came to set us free. Jesus sets us free from selfishness and sin so we can become all God created us to be: the-very-best-version-of-ourselves.

Jesus says you are a child of God, you are infinitely valuable, and you are free—and Jesus' opinion matters.

•●●•

Who do people say that Jesus is? Who do you say that Jesus is? Who does Jesus say that you are? These are three questions worthy of our attention.

Jesus wants us to be very clear about who he is, because being clear about who he is allows us to become clear about who we are. Our identity is inextricably tied to Jesus.

The more we discover who Jesus truly is, the more we will place him at the center of our lives. It is the only sane response to knowing him. The more we place Jesus at the center of our lives, the more life begins to make sense. It is simply impossible to make sense of life without the clarity that comes from placing Jesus at the center. I have tried this foolishness and I have failed. You can try if you wish, but you will fail too.

POINT TO PONDER: No matter what happens, God loves you.

VERSE TO LIVE: "Am I now seeking human approval or God's approval? Or am I trying to please people? If I were still pleasing people, I would not be a servant of Christ." GALATIANS 1:10

QUESTION TO CONSIDER: Do you value yourself anywhere near as much as Jesus values you?

PRAYER: Jesus, thank you for revealing yourself to me. Thank you for all you have done for me. Thank you for loving me even more than I love myself.

EIGHT

Jesus Was a Radical

JESUS HAS A VISION FOR YOUR LIFE.

Open up your Bible and read one of the four Gospels from start to finish. Try to do it with fresh eyes, and you will be struck by something: Jesus was a radical—and his life and teachings are a radical invitation to something beyond what most of us have settled for in our everyday lives.

What does *radical* mean? It means to get to the "root" of things.

Jesus was interested in getting deep down to the root of things. He was interested in what was essential—not the fluffy periphery, but the core, the center, the heart of things.

Jesus wasn't trapped by the notion of political correctness. He wasn't burdened with the need to be liked by people. He wasn't moved by the desire for expediency or convenience. Instead, he simply allowed truth to reign supreme.

Truth is radical.

To abide completely by the truth in every situation in our lives is incredibly difficult. It requires both the heart of a saint and the diplomacy of an experienced ambassador. Every day we are tempted in dozens of ways to have a casual relationship with truth. Many situations emerge each week in which we are tempted to ignore the truth, or bend it, stretch it, or massage it, out of political correctness, a desire to be liked, expediency, or convenience.

But Jesus didn't have a casual relationship with truth, and that is radical. He was interested in getting to the root of things. Through this lens of truth Jesus places everything in its proper place, bringing order to every aspect of life, and demonstrates the true value of things. We all yearn for this divine ordering. The challenge is to surrender and allow God to put our lives in order. The fruit of this surrender is the peace and joy that we all desire.

Jesus was a radical. He reminds us at every turn that God's ways are not a slight variation of man's ways, but that they are in fact radically different. Embrace any *one* of Jesus' teachings seriously and some of the people around you are bound to think that you are taking it a little too far. His teachings don't invite us to the mediocre middle. They invite us to a radical love.

This radical love is at the heart of the Gospel. There are of course spectacular displays, but most of all Jesus invites us to pass this radical love along to others through the daily events of our lives. At every turn Jesus mentors us in this radical love.

Jesus was a radical. His life was radical. His death was radical. His teachings were radical. They got to the root of things. His love was radical. It changed the entire course of human history.

POINT TO PONDER: Ask Jesus to help you get to the root of things in your life. Ask him to help you embrace the truth.

VERSE TO LIVE: "Let the same mind be in you that was in Christ Jesus." PHILIPPIANS 2:5

QUESTION TO CONSIDER: When was the last time you had the courage to seek out the root of an important issue?

PRAYER: Jesus, point me toward the root of things, and give me an extra nudge when I am tempted to settle for the shallow and the superficial.

NINE
The Greatest Teacher Ever

SIMPLE IS NOT THE SAME AS EASY.

People often confuse simple for easy. Jesus' teachings were radically simple. Experts have a special talent for complicating things. But the stand-out genius in any field is always the person who is able to take what is incredibly complex, break it down to what is essential, and present it in a way that makes it seem simple.

Spiritual leaders of all types throughout history have often complicated the path to God in ways that have made it almost impossible for the average person to walk the path. God gave Moses the Ten Commandments. By the time of Jesus, these had evolved into 613 laws. The simplicity of Jesus' teaching was radical in contrast to the stifling effect these 613 laws had on daily life.

Jesus' teachings were radical in content and method. But they also provide unique insight into the mind of God. In many ways reading the Gospels is a tour through the mind of God. Each parable or teaching, each encounter Jesus has with a person highlights what God cares about and what he doesn't. The life and teachings of Jesus Christ help us to understand God's priorities, so that we can get our own priorities right.

The content of his teachings was radical because it focused on conversion of the heart rather than external behaviors. The method of his teachings was radical because his primary teaching tool was the parable. He used stories and metaphors that ordinary people could understand. This meant that his teachings were accessible and practical to ordinary people, especially the uneducated.

The Gospel may be difficult to live, but it is unrelentingly simple in its teaching. The Gospel is radically simple, and there is genius in its simplicity.

What Jesus taught was radical, and how he taught was also radical. The four Gospels contain rare insights into the genius of the mind of God. Realizing this changes the way we read the Gospels.

As we ponder the various situations and circumstances of Jesus' life and reflect on his words and actions, it becomes clear what he was doing. He was constantly trying to get to the root of every situation, to explore the root of every problem, to expose and transform the root of each person's heart.

But to discover the Gospels in this way, we have to ponder them. This is different from just reading them. It's different from just listening to them in church on Sunday. By definition, *ponder* means "to consider something deeply, thoroughly; to meditate upon." To *meditate* means "to engage in a spiritual exercise for the purpose of reaching a heightened level of spiritual awareness."

Where is this in our lives? Who around you is striving for a heightened level of spiritual awareness?

I'll tell you who had it: Mary. We read in Luke's Gospel, "Mary treasured all these things and pondered them in her heart" (Luke 2:19). What was she pondering? She was pondering the happenings of Jesus' life. Mary was the first to ponder the Gospel. She witnessed the life and teachings of Jesus unfolding before her very eyes: the ordinary and the radical.

Jesus' life was radical and beautiful, and his teachings are radical and beautiful.

What was his most radical teaching? We could debate this question endlessly, but one of the great dangers when it comes to Jesus and his teachings is to depersonalize the conversation. So perhaps a better question to explore would be: Which of Jesus' teachings do you find it most difficult to live?

Jesus isn't just a teacher; he is the greatest teacher who ever lived. He isn't just a genius; he *is* genius. His words are the most influential in history. We each discover that for ourselves when we open our hearts and minds to how those words are inviting us to change.

POINT TO PONDER: Jesus wants to teach you how to live an incredible life.

VERSE TO LIVE: "Everyone who listens to these words of mine and acts on them will be like a wise man who built his house upon rock." MATTHEW 7:24

QUESTION TO CONSIDER: Have you ever really considered Jesus to be your teacher?

PRAYER: Jesus, teach me how to be a great student.

TEN

Forty Words

GOD SEES THINGS IN YOU that you don't see in yourself.

Jesus was teaching one day in the synagogue when he was asked, "Which is the greatest of the commandments?" The question was a trap. At the time of Jesus, there were 613 laws. These laws were meant to protect people from breaking the Ten Commandments. But many Jewish people were so fixated on the laws that they lost sight of the central teachings of the Torah and the heart of God's message.

And yet, Jesus cuts through the complexity. With the clarity, power, and genius of simplicity, he perfectly summarizes the Gospel. This was Jesus' response: "'You shall love the Lord your God with all your heart, with all your soul, and with all your mind.' This is the greatest and first commandment. And the second is like it: 'You shall love your neighbor as yourself'" (Matthew 22:39).

In forty words Jesus gives us a mini-Gospel. In forty words he gives us a mini-examination of conscience. In forty words he says, "If you are looking for something to measure your life by, use this!"

But perhaps what is most radical here is also what is most often overlooked. It may also be one of the hardest aspects of the Christian faith to live. In these lines, Jesus invites us to a total love of God and a generous love of neighbor, but he assumes that we already love ourselves. "You shall love your neighbor as yourself." There is a connection between our ability to love ourselves in a healthy way and our ability to love our neighbor. This is a major stumbling block for many of us as Christians. It is a generalization, but my experience leads me to conclude that many Christians do a horrible job of loving themselves. We are wrapped up in a self-loathing that is unhealthy. We are constantly judging ourselves in ways that are unproductive. We are often less willing to forgive ourselves than God is to forgive us. On the surface, of course, we pretend otherwise. But Jesus is not interested in the surface. He wants to drive deep down to the root of things.

I am not speaking of the love of self that is blind and boastful, but rather the love of self that acknowledges that we are weak and wounded, and at the same time that we are amazing children of God. It's that unique combination of humility and gratitude that allows us to acknowledge (even if we don't understand it) that God loves us deeply, that he loves us for a reason, and that that alone is proof that we are lovable.

We are lovable. You are lovable.

I have traveled the world more than most people, and the amount of self-loathing that we seem to have for ourselves as Christians never ceases to break my heart. Our inability to love ourselves may be one of the biggest problems in the Church today. For until we learn to love ourselves as God wants us to, our ability to love others will be limited and deformed.

When we love ourselves we become less interested in what others think about us and more interested in what God thinks. When we love ourselves we don't do things just to get noticed or praised or accepted.

Here is a practical example: How many gifts did you give to others last year? Most of us give dozens of gifts to other people every year: birthdays, Christmas, weddings, anniversaries, etc. These gifts are given to friends, family, colleagues, and perhaps even strangers. If we give a gift with love of self in our hearts, we do it because we want to, and we don't have any expectations. Sure, we hope people like the gifts we give them, but whether they do or not, we know it was a thoughtful and generous thing to do. We cannot control the way another person responds to a gift—only the way the gift is given.

If we give a gift *without* a healthy self-love, we may or may not be doing it because we actually want to. A gift given without self-love comes with expectations. When we give such a gift we want the recipient to thank us, praise us, like us, favor us. In this case, we will only feel good about giving the gift if the recipient responds in exactly the way we want him or her to. If the recipient doesn't like the gift, we will be disappointed and our sense of self will be diminished, because we gave the gift hoping for love and acceptance in return.

A healthy sense of self-love is essential to the life of a Christian. God desires it for you. This self-love can coexist with true humility.

God wants you to be very clear that you are as important as anyone else. Any thought that you don't matter, that others are more important than you, that your thoughts or feelings are not valid, or that people will not like you unless you please them are not from God. These are not thoughts that come from the mind of God.

Learn to love yourself. That's radical. Your ability to love yourself will have a direct impact on your ability to love God and to love your neighbor. That is radical and profound.

POINT TO PONDER: God wants to raise you up.

VERSE TO LIVE: "As God's chosen ones, holy, and beloved, clothe yourselves with compassion, kindness, humility, meekness, and patience." COLOSSIANS 3:12

QUESTION TO CONSIDER: Are you loving yourself the way God wants you to love yourself?

PRAYER: Jesus, begin a revolution of love in my heart today. Teach me to love myself as you love me, so that I can love all those who cross my path in a way that reminds them that you changed the world.

ELEVEN

The Heart of the Gospel

GIVE AND FORGIVE.

Generosity and forgiveness are two of the most radical invitations the Gospel makes. They are also among the most difficult to live.

"Whoever has two coats must share with anyone who has none; and whoever has food must do likewise" (Luke 3:11).

This passage deals with generosity. In the next section we will explore forgiveness.

Jesus wants you to become the most generous person in your sphere of influence. He wants you to astonish people with your generosity. He wants you to be generous with your time, talent, and treasure. But he invites you to a generosity that goes far beyond these. He wants you to be generous with your praise and encouragement. He wants you to be generous with your compassion and patience. He wants generosity to reach into every area of your life so that through you he can love and intrigue the people in your life.

Open your wardrobe. How many coats do you have? How many shirts and sweaters are in there? How many pairs of pants and shoes do you have? When was the last time you even wore some of that stuff?

What was Jesus saying? If you have more than you need, be generous to those who don't have what they need. You have heard it said, God provides for humanity's need, not for humanity's greed.

Jesus' notion of generosity is radical. I am not a scholar of early Christian life, but it seems to me that one of the reasons Christianity thrived in those early days was because the generosity of the first Christians intrigued people. Christian generosity is radical, especially when it was lived out in contrast to the brutally harsh climate of self-interest of the first century.

Ever since that time, followers of Jesus have been astonishing the people of every age with their generosity. It is the generosity that naturally springs forth when we wholeheartedly embrace the teachings of Jesus Christ.

The Gospel liberates us from selfishness by inspiring us to be generous. Great lives belong to men and women who see life as a generosity contest. Decide right now, here, today, to live a life of staggering generosity. Astonish the people who cross your path with your generosity. There may be no more practical way to bring Christianity to life.

POINT TO PONDER: Generosity is incredibly attractive.

VERSE TO LIVE: "Some give freely, yet grow all the richer; others withhold what is due, and only suffer want. A generous person will be enriched, and one who gives water will get water."
PROVERBS 11:24–25

QUESTION TO CONSIDER: How is God inviting you to become more generous?

PRAYER: Jesus, liberate me from any inclination to be stingy.

TWELVE

The Soul of the Gospel

THERE CAN BE NO PEACE without forgiveness.

Forgiveness is one of the central lessons in the life and teachings of Jesus. It plays a powerful role in the spiritual health of every person. It also plays a powerful role in every relationship, and it is essential to the life of any healthy community, whether that community is as small as a family or as large as a nation.

When we forgive, we share the love of God with others and rid ourselves of dangerous poisons that can prevent us from growing spiritually. But that doesn't make it easy.

"Then Peter came to Jesus and asked, 'How many times shall I forgive a brother or sister who has sinned against me? As many as seven times?' Jesus said to him, 'Not seven times, but seventy-seven times'" (Matthew 18:21).

Without forgiveness our souls begin to fill with anger, resentment, frustration, and anxiety. Choosing not to forgive someone is like drinking poison and expecting the other person to die. When we choose not to forgive, we turn our backs on God and the-best-version-of-ourselves.

Everybody needs to forgive somebody. Whom do you need to forgive? Whom is God inviting you to forgive?

Forgiveness is also a powerful countercultural element of Christianity.

While Jesus' teaching was and is radical, he calls us beyond forgiveness. One of his most radical teachings is: "Love your enemies and pray for those who persecute you" (Matthew 5:44). What was the teaching before Jesus wandered into the synagogue that morning? "An eye for an eye, and a tooth for a tooth" (Exodus 21:24).

We may have read or heard this reading from Matthew's Gospel many times. But the moment Jesus proclaimed this teaching was actually one of the great moral, ethical, and spiritual advances in human history. Jesus outlawed revenge and vengeance with one sentence.

What is he saying? He is saying love Emperor Nero, Adolf Hitler, Osama bin Laden, and child molesters, and pray for them. This teaching is so radical that when we really stop to think about it, our chests get tight, the airways to our lungs become constricted, and we find it hard to breathe.

Who are your enemies? When was the last time you prayed for them? There are some people who say they don't have any enemies. They simply have not thought it through. Who are the people on television who make your skin crawl and your blood boil? Who represents ideas that are at the other end of the ideological spectrum from everything that you hold to be good, true, noble, and just? These people are your enemies. When was the last time you prayed for them?

Radical, huh?

And let's not forget the everyday ways people wrong you. They cut you off in traffic, jump in front of you to get through the express lane at the supermarket with fifty-seven items, or say things about you that are not true.

Forgiveness and generosity are two of the most radical challenges Jesus levels at us. They are at once incredibly spiritual and monumentally practical. Our willingness to give and forgive often reveals the depth, or limitations, of our Christianity.

POINT TO PONDER: Everybody needs to forgive somebody.

VERSE TO LIVE: "If you forgive others their trespasses, your heavenly father will also forgive you." MATTHEW 6:14

QUESTION TO CONSIDER: How seriously do you take Jesus' invitation to forgive?

PRAYER: Jesus, you forgive me even though you know I am going to sin again. Teach me to be that generous with my forgiveness.

THIRTEEN
Who Is the Greatest?

JESUS' TEACHINGS ARE A PARADOX to our worldly thinking.

"At that time the disciples came to Jesus and asked, 'Who is
the greatest in the kingdom of heaven?' He called a child, whom
he put among them, and said, 'Truly I tell you, unless you change
and become like little children, you will never enter the kingdom
of heaven'" (Matthew 18:1–3).

Jesus' whole attitude toward children was radical. To understand just how radical Jesus' teaching about children were, it is
essential to delve into the way children were treated and viewed
at that time. When Jesus taught that we are all children of God,
he was announcing that every child (or person) is of equal inesti-
mable value in the eyes of God. This was astonishing to the Jews,
who saw themselves as the chosen people. It was also astonishing to the secular authorities of the time. In the Roman Empire
your value as a child was based in large part on your parentage.
If your father was a king, then you were a treasure to the nation,
especially if you were a male. Other than parentage, the value of
children was determined by their ability to serve the state.

At the time of Jesus, all children were not considered equal. Women were generally shut off from education and public life, and many grew up to be slaves. The empire had an insatiable need for labor, and women and children were often the slaves who filled this need.

Even more horrifying was the practice of "exposure," which involved abandoning a newborn child in a secluded area, often a dump or dung hill, and allowing her to die from lack of food and care, ravaged by animals or the elements. Sometimes abandoned children were rescued, but usually by opportunists who were looking to raise them to sell them as slaves. During those times the head of the household had the legal right to decide the life or death of a child, especially during the first eight days of life. The reasons children were exposed included poverty or inability to provide for the child, disability or deformity, the desire of a wealthy family to avoid dividing the estate, wrong gender (males were valued more than females), and illegitimacy. The earliest followers of Jesus became known for their radical love because they rescued these abandoned children, took them into their homes, and cared for them.

We have come a long way, primarily because of the way Jesus' teachings transformed how we view children. When Jesus said things like, "Let the little children come to me" (Matthew 19:4), it wasn't just a cute gesture; he was turning social structures upside down. He was boldly announcing: Children are important; children matter.

When Jesus announced that we are all children of God, he threatened the social and economic structures of his time. The same teaching challenges those structures today. If we truly believed that the children starving in our own country and around the world were God's children, how would we behave differently? If we actually believed that women being persecuted and suppressed around the world were our sisters, what would we do about it? If we are all children of God, and the shoes we wear are sewn together by a child in a foreign country who should be at school, not at work, and is being paid less than it costs to simply survive, what is our moral responsibility?

The Gospel of Jesus Christ is a radical invitation to get beyond our own self-centered worldview and do our part to protect and liberate the most vulnerable children of God. In doing this it is also important to remember that some of God's most vulnerable children are adults. Jesus teaches us, "Whatever you did for one of these least brothers of mine, you did for me" (Matthew 25: 40). Lines like these are haunting if you really reflect on them.

The Gospels turn our social structure upside down by announcing that we are all children of God, and therefore, we are all sons and daughters of a great king. God wants us to embrace our identity as his sons and daughters, and then recognize that same identity in every person we encounter. It is a difficult lesson.

The culture is full of identity confusion. As a parent I am constantly vigilant regarding the identity my children are taking on as a result of daily interaction with other people and the culture. I want my children to know that they are children of a great king, God. I made a poster to hang in my daughter's room that reads:

"I am the daughter of a great king. He is my father and my God. The world may praise me or criticize me. It matters not. He is with me, always at my side, guiding and protecting me. I do not fear because I am his."

In the boys' room, there is the same poster with just a couple of changes: "I am the son of a great king..."

The divine social structure is radically different from the one we experience every day. Think about Christianity next time you take a trip. Those who travel a lot and have elite status with airlines and hotel chains receive special privileges. They are treated like kings and queens, with upgrades to first class on flights and great suites in hotels. They get to check in first, board first, avoid long security lines, enjoy free meals and beverages, and more. This is the way of the world.

Now imagine if Jesus owned an airline. The pre-boarding announcement would be: "Ladies and gentleman, welcome to Jesus Air. We do things differently here. We are delighted that you are joining us and we are looking forward to serving you so that you can have an incredible experience. At Jesus Air we board by zones. Zone 1 consists of those with absolutely no status in this world, the lowest of the low on the frequent-flyer totem pole. Zone 2 consists of our Silver members. Zone 3 is for our Gold members. Zone 4 will consist of our Platinum members. And finally Zone 5, in which there are only middle seats left and absolutely no overhead space for your carry-ons, is for those overprivileged, constantly pampered Diamond members. At Jesus Air our motto is the first shall be last and the last shall be first. Thank you for flying Jesus Air."

We all enjoy VIP service, but Jesus tells us that the least among us deserve it too. Who are the least among you? How are you treating them? Jesus tells us that we should be giving them preferential treatment. Sobering, isn't it? Radical.

Jesus teaches us to give preferential treatment to the poor. Let's take a look at a story that he told that haunts me. It is about Lazarus, the poor man who sat at the rich man's door begging for scraps from the rich man's table. The rich man died and Jesus conveyed this conversation from the afterlife: "'Father Abraham, have mercy on me, and send Lazarus to dip the tip of his finger in water and cool my tongue; for I am in agony in these flames.' But Abraham said, 'Child, remember that during your lifetime you received your good things, and Lazarus in like manner evil things; but now he is comforted here and you are in agony'" (Luke 16:14–15).

This one scares me. Like the rich man, I get to enjoy many of the good things life has to offer. The poor may not be sitting on my doorstep, but they are not far from it. This story makes my soul tremble, because Jesus clearly speaks about an afterlife and a place that I have no interest in spending time. He also makes a connection between the way we live our lives here on earth and where we end up in the afterlife.

The Gospels inform us of our serious and inescapable obligation to the poor. It is impossible to separate the spiritual teachings of Jesus Christ from his social teachings, just as it is impossible to separate our love of God from our love of neighbor. The dual command to love God and love neighbor are inseparable. It is easy to say, "I love God." It is easy to say, "I am a Christian." But Jesus challenges us to prove it. Our love of neighbor is the proof that we love God.

POINT TO PONDER: The poor, the needy, the hungry, the lonely, the ignorant, and the afflicted are God's special friends.

VERSE TO LIVE: "Live justly, love tenderly, and walk humbly with your God." MICAH 6:8

QUESTION TO CONSIDER: Do your values align with Jesus' values?

PRAYER: Jesus, set the child within me free so I can be more childlike with every passing day, and open the eyes of my soul that I may see your children all around me.

FOURTEEN
Purity of Heart

GOD WANTS YOU TO BE master of what you choose to look at.

"Everyone who looks at a woman with lust has already committed adultery with her in his heart" (Matthew 5:28). This is a radical teaching. When was the last time you looked at a man or a woman lustfully? Jesus calls this adultery of the heart.

Our sight is an incredible gift from God. The Gospel invites us to practice custody of the eyes, which simply means having the self-control to decide what we allow ourselves to look at. In our hypersexual culture we are constantly being visually harassed by sexual images. This makes maintaining custody of the eyes a constant struggle. Some things we look at help us become the-best-version-of-ourselves, and others don't. Having custody of the eyes means exercising the self-control to not look at the things that don't help us become the-best-version-of-ourselves.

Sometimes it all depends on the way you look at something. If a bunch of guys are standing around and they notice a beautiful woman walking by, it is one thing to acknowledge her beauty as a gift from God. It is something else entirely if they turn around and follow her with their eyes and let their imaginations run wild.

Images are powerful. You cannot unsee things. Edit what you look at. Custody of the eyes is a sure path to spiritual growth.

POINT TO PONDER: Avert your eyes from anything that can pollute your soul.

VERSE TO LIVE: "The eye is the lamp of the body. So, if your eye is sound your whole body will be full of light." MATTHEW 6:22

QUESTION TO CONSIDER: If you learn to control what you look at, how deep will the peace within you be?

PRAYER: Jesus, purify my heart, purify my mind, purify my body, and purify my soul.

FIFTEEN
Making Sense of Suffering

WE ALL SUFFER.

When my dad died I was sad. It hurt. The pain was like a dull ache that just wouldn't go away. I wanted to have just one more good conversation with him. I missed him and I knew I would continue to miss him. I knew he would never get to meet my wife and children, and I knew there would be many key moments in my life when I would yearn for him to be there.

I was sad for my younger brothers, especially Hamish, my youngest. I was thirty years old when Dad died, but Hamish was only twenty-two and he had lived with Dad through almost five years of illness. So Dad had been sick since Hamish was about seventeen, and that is too young to lose your father.

Suffering comes in many shapes and sizes, and wears many masks. The first time I was diagnosed with cancer, I remember walking out of the doctor's office. My ears were ringing and everything seemed to be a blur. All around me people were just getting on with their lives, but my life had changed in an instant. Being sick yourself is a different type of sadness and a different type of suffering.

When my brother Mark died, it was different again. It was different from my dad dying and different from having cancer. Mark was in the prime of his life. He had two daughters and a wife who needed him. When my dad died it was sad, but he had lived a full life. My brother left too much of life unlived, and his death hurt more because of that.

There are other types of suffering that I dread. I dread the pain that comes from helplessly watching someone I love suffer, knowing there is absolutely nothing I can do. I dread having to see my own children suffer. When my son Walter was about one he had severe asthma, and one night we had to take him to the emergency room. I ended up spending the night in the hospital with him, but the whole floor he was on was full of sick children. Many of them had been there for weeks or months, and some of them were never going home again.

Suffering is one of the central mysteries of the human experience. I don't know why I suffer in certain ways and you suffer in other ways. I don't know why some people's suffering is very public, and other people suffer quietly and inwardly in ways that nobody else would ever know. I don't know why my brother died in the prime of his life. It doesn't make sense to me. It's a mystery—and I have learned to make peace with life's mysteries.

I am not fool enough to believe that my finite mind can comprehend the infinite mind of God. Faith and hope lead me to the conclusion that suffering has value. I do not fully understand the reason or the value of suffering. Suffering is a mystery—and I am OK with that. Mystery is a beautiful thing. It shouldn't be scoffed at, but rather should be approached with reverence and awe.

The cross is central to the life of Jesus. His suffering had unfathomable value. I believe that our suffering is connected to his suffering in ways we will never fully understand in this lifetime. And in the next life we may discover that suffering in this life was in fact a great honor. We just don't know. It's a mystery—and I am OK with that.

Suffering is an inevitable part of life, but it doesn't have to be meaningless. Like so many things in life that we have little or no control over, how we respond to suffering makes all the difference.

Jesus counsels us:

> I tell you, you will weep and mourn, but the world will rejoice; you will have pain, but your pain will turn into joy. When a woman is in labor, she has pain, because her hour has come. But when her child is born, she no longer remembers the anguish because of the joy of having brought a human being into the world. So you have pain now; but I will see you again, and your hearts will rejoice, and no one will take your joy from you. (John 16:20–22)

This passage alone is proof enough that Jesus sees suffering in a completely different light than the world does, and that his conception of suffering is radically different from how I would view it if I were left to my own devices. Fortunately for us all, Jesus doesn't leave us to our own devices.

Suffering reminds us, perhaps more than anything else, that God's ways are not ours. We live in a secular culture that despises suffering as useless and proclaims that it should be avoided at all costs. As a result, pain relievers are constantly being thrust at us in the form of pills, products, experiences, and distractions.

The world has its own gospel. The message of the world is incomplete, and nothing demonstrates this incompleteness more than the world's inability to make sense of suffering. The world cannot make sense of suffering because it views suffering as worthless. The world has no answer for the inescapable, unavoidable, and inevitable suffering of our lives.

Jesus has an answer for everything.

The Old Testament Scriptures tell us that suffering is the consequence of sin. In the Old Testament suffering is presented as a punishment inflicted by God as a direct result of humanity's sinfulness. In the New Testament, Jesus boldly announced with his words and actions that suffering has value. It is a tool that can transform us into more loving people. It ushers us into higher spiritual realms. Salvation and the suffering of Jesus are inseparable. So what could be more meaningful than suffering?

Now, let's be very clear. I am not suggesting that we should go looking for suffering. And there is a great deal of suffering in this world that you and I can and should do more to relieve. But the inescapable suffering of our lives has a purpose. We can try to run from it, or we can accept it and allow it to transform us in unimaginable ways. We can allow it to make us angry, or we can let it teach us how to love more fully.

For hundreds of years Christians have whispered to each other, "Offer it up!" The Scriptures encourage us to offer everything that happens in our day—the joys and suffering—to God as a prayer. Suffering is a powerful prayer. Once we come to this realization and begin to surrender to the inevitable suffering of life, offering it to God as a prayer—for ourselves, for our friends and family, for the world—we become filled with a deep and abiding peace.

Jesus promised us suffering. His leadership was unique and awesome; he didn't sugarcoat things or pretend. He led by example and asked for great commitment from those who wanted to follow him.

For more than two thousand years, the heroes, champions, and saints of Christianity have been meditating on the passion and death of Jesus Christ. Perhaps it is time we all spent a little time exploring the genius of the cross. The world changed at three o'clock on that Friday afternoon when Jesus laid down his life for us. That was how he changed the world. Radical.

"If any want to become my followers, let them deny themselves and take up their cross daily and follow me" (Luke 9:23).

The mandate is clear. I don't know what your cross is, but I sure know what my own is. Some days I am more reluctant than others to pick it up and carry it. That's life. What cross is Jesus inviting you to take up and carry today? Whatever it is, the risen Christ wants to help you carry it. You are not alone.

POINT TO PONDER: Suffering transforms us in unimaginable ways.

VERSE TO LIVE: "We rejoice in our sufferings, knowing that suffering produces endurance and endurance produces character, and character produces hope." ROMANS 5:3–4

QUESTION TO CONSIDER: Are you willing to suffer a little in order to grow spiritually?

PRAYER: Jesus, teach me to embrace the unavoidable suffering of life, and keep me ever mindful of those who suffer more than I do.

SIXTEEN

Do Not Judge

GOD WANTS TO EMPTY YOUR heart of judgment.

Do not judge, so that you may not be judged. For with the
judgment you make you will be judged, and the measure you
give will be the measure you get. Why do you see the speck
in your neighbor's eye, but do not notice the log in your own
eye? Or how can you say to your neighbor, 'Let me take the
speck out of your eye,' while the log is in your own eye? You
hypocrite, first take the log out of your own eye, and then
you will see clearly to take the speck out of your neighbor's
eye. (Matthew 7:1–5)

Judgment is one of the major obstacles that prevent us from loving others as God commands us to. It is also an obstacle in our
quest to love ourselves as God wants us to.

I wish I could tell you that I have so fully embraced Jesus'
teachings that I never judge anyone, but I can't. I catch myself

judging people all the time. I waste so much time and energy judging, and it makes me unhappy. When I judge others I hurt them, I create negativity, I feel bad about myself, and I am more likely to judge myself in unhealthy ways.

"Do not judge." Now, that is a radical invitation.

We live in a hyper-opinionated culture. As a result of all these opinions, we have become hyper-judgmental. All this judgment is unhealthy and unchristian. How many times a day do you judge other people? How many times a day do you judge yourself? Let me recommend an immensely practical spiritual exercise: Count. For twenty-four hours, count how many times you judge something or someone.

At every turn Jesus' teachings provide practical ways to grow spiritually. Just focusing on reducing the amount of judgment in your life is a path to peace, joy, and incredible spiritual growth. You will immediately experience the internal fruit of this path through a new peace that will flood your soul. But you will also quickly discover the external impact reducing judgment has on relationships.

Nobody likes being around someone who is constantly judging them. Our relationships cannot survive under the unbearable weight of constant judgment. When we stop pumping the poison of judgment into the greenhouses of our relationships, we all begin to thrive in a new way together.

It is simply not our place to judge. To judge is a divine prerogative. A prerogative is, an exclusive right or privilege. To judge is God's exclusive right. Throughout history humanity has been pretending to be God in a thousand different ways, and this always leads to problems. When we fill our hearts and minds with judgment, this is just one more arrogant and futile attempt to pretend that we are God.

Even Jesus was not spared the arrogance of human judgment. His actions and motives were constantly being questioned: "Why does he eat with tax collectors and sinners?" (Mark 2:16).

One of our favorite ways to judge other people is by giving them labels. "He's too conservative." "She's a liberal." "She is friends with *those* people." "He lives on *that* street." "They belong to *that* club." "They are not really your type of people." "His child is the one who . . ." "He went to *that* school."

It all seems very innocent, as if we are just conveying facts, but that is how insidious our judging has become.

•●◆●•

Jesus' teaching on judging is just one example of the practical and profound nature of his teachings. This one teaching could change your life. This one teaching could change the world.

Did Jesus misspeak? I don't think so. He spoke with abundant clarity in a way that challenged people to their core two thousand years ago, and in a way that continues to challenge people to their core two thousand years later.

We can put up barriers and make excuses. We can argue about exactly what he meant by this saying or that. But somewhere deep inside I think most of us know that he is calling us to live differently. Not for his sake, but for ours. Not to make him happy, but so that we can share in the happiness that is our destiny.

The teachings of Jesus Christ are radical. For two thousand years men and women of all ages, from all walks of life—rich and poor, young and old, educated and uneducated—have been allowing these teachings to transform them. Now the question is, will you?

POINT TO PONDER: Whenever you are tempted to judge someone, turn your attention to seeing that person as a child of God.

VERSE TO LIVE: "Who are you to judge your neighbor?"
JAMES 4:12

QUESTION TO CONSIDER: How will your key relationships improve if they are free from judgment?

PRAYER: Jesus, make me aware just before I am about to fall into judging someone, and give me the grace to stop myself.

SEVENTEEN
Radical Relationships

GOD LOVES EVEN THOSE WHO seem unlovable.

There are many dimensions to Jesus the radical. Yes, his teachings were radical, but his desire to be a radical influence extended far beyond his teachings. Let's consider the radical nature of his daily interactions with people.

Most of the people who are at the center of the Gospel narrative have no place in our lives. What does that tell us? Jesus took people whom you and I would mindlessly pass on the street, people we would never choose to be in the same room with, people from the very margins of society, and he placed them at the center of the narrative we call the Gospel. They came to him in a hundred guises—the sick, the poor, the despised, women, children, and sinners of every type—but in each of them Jesus saw a child of God.

There is perhaps no more powerful example of this than the woman at the well: "A Samaritan woman came to draw water, and Jesus said to her, 'Give me a drink.' [His disciples had gone to the city to buy food.] The Samaritan woman said to him, 'How is it that you, a Jew, ask a drink of me, a woman of Samaria?'" (John 4:7–8).

Everyone—the Jews, the gentiles, the Romans—despised the Samaritans. So what did Jesus do? He gave them a central place in the Gospel. First, there is the Good Samaritan parable, which has made the name Samaritan synonymous with good work and mercy. For two thousand years every kind act toward a stranger has carried the good Samaritan name (see Luke 10:25–37).

Then, here in this story, Jesus encountered not just a Samaritan, but a Samaritan woman, and not just a Samaritan woman, but a Samaritan woman who had been divorced several times. Jesus was truly on the fringes of the social structure when he decided to strike up a conversation with this woman. Even her own people looked down on her. The stigma attached to this woman was monumental, making the lesson all the more powerful.

Did Jesus just politely say hello to her? No. Did he have a shallow conversation with her? No. This is the longest recorded conversation between Jesus and any other human being.

Think about that.

Jesus' attitude toward people was radically different because he saw in every man, woman, and child a child of God.

We could talk more about the various and unlikely people Jesus spent his time with, but I think the point is well made. He made a radical choice to spend time with people on the fringes of society, and his interactions with them were radical.

Jesus also had a close circle of friends, the people he did life with. And whom he chose for his inner circle is another example of the radical way he did things.

In those days he departed to the mountain to pray, and he spent the night in prayer to God. When day came, he called his disciples to himself, and from them he chose Twelve, whom he also named apostles: Simon, whom he named Peter, and his brother Andrew, James, John, Philip, Bartholomew, Matthew, Thomas, James the son of Alphaeus, Simon who was called a Zealot, and Judas the son of James, and Judas Iscariot, who became a traitor. (Luke 6:12–16)

If Jesus had come to you and said, "These are the twelve guys I have chosen to change the world," you probably would have questioned his judgment. The disciples were an unlikely group of men, not the all-star leadership team that most of us would want if our intention were to start a movement that would transform the entire world and everyone in it in every imaginable way. Sure, the Gospel is primarily a call to spiritual transformation, but the implications of that spiritual transformation reach into every corner of life and society.

Jesus completely rejected the social norms of the day when he chose the people he spent time with. And I suspect he would do the same if he were alive today. What does that teach us about the people we spend our time with?

There are two lessons here for us. First, we all need a group of people to do life with—people who walk with us through the good and the bad, who encourage and challenge us to be the-best-version-of-ourselves.

Second, Jesus made a habit of going out of his way to engage people on the fringe of society. He didn't spend all his time with them. He had his close friends and inner circle. The point is he never avoided people on the edge of society, and in fact even willingly encountered them.

Where are these people in your life?

The Gospels are an invitation to explore all of life, to get beyond the comfortable center of life and explore the margins. The parts of life we avoid and ignore are the very parts that Jesus was most interested in. The types of people we avoid and ignore are the types of people Jesus was most interested in.

What does that say about our lives? How does that invite us to change? What prevents us from changing? What are we afraid of? And have we even considered the other side of the question? Rather than always framing it negatively, what are the positive possibilities that might come about if we open ourselves to more fully embrace the Gospel?

POINT TO PONDER: Every person is as important and valuable as the person you consider most important and valuable.

VERSE TO LIVE: "Give justice to the weak and the orphan; maintain the right of the lowly and the destitute. Rescue the weak and the needy." PSALM 82:3–4

QUESTION TO CONSIDER: What is God saying to you through this teaching today?

PRAYER: Jesus, open my eyes so I can see every person I encounter each day as you see them.

EIGHTEEN

Jesus on Lifestyle

PEOPLE ARE A PRIORITY FOR GOD.

People were made to be loved, and things were made to be used. But often we get this confused and many of the world's problems are caused because we love things and use people.

If you want to take a good, honest look at what your priorities are, get out your checkbook and credit card statement and examine the things you spend money on. Still not sure? Then get out your planner or calendar and explore the things you give your time to.

Do we have Jesus' priorities? Are we living Gospel values? The answer is usually yes and no. We do and are, to some extent, but there is still a lot of work to be done.

The world is constantly trying to seduce us to make things, money, accomplishments, and comfort the priorities of our lives. And we have all worshipped these things to varying extents by giving them an inordinate place in our lives.

So once again Jesus challenges us to rethink everything surrounding the way we live.

Things and People

You have heard it said that the best things in life are not things. So what are the best things in life? What are the best things in your life right now? And what are the best things that are not in your life yet because you don't even know that they should be?

A lot of our modern lifestyle is based on having things. Jesus rejected the idea that things should have a primary place in our lives. Other than the clothes on his back and the sandals on his feet, he had nothing. And his teachings constantly affirmed that people were primary and things were secondary.

Our collective lust for money and things has blinded us to the real and legitimate needs of so many people. Some of these people live just a few blocks from us. Others live on the other side of the world. All are children of God, and that makes them our brothers and sisters.

The problem is we value some people more than other people. Jesus doesn't do that. If a hundred people died in a natural disaster in our city, this would capture our attention for days, weeks, months, or even years. If a thousand people died on the other side of the world, we might barely think of it again after watching the story on the news.

Why do we value American lives more than African lives? Why are we comfortable with Asian children sewing our running shoes in horrific conditions for wages that are barely enough to buy food? What is so important? Cheap shoes. Cheap clothes. Cheap drill bits. Cheap stuff.

Would you be willing to pay a little more? How much more? Our quest for more and more of everything is affecting real lives.

Our quest for the cheapest of everything is literally killing people in other parts of the world. Those people over there, in other countries, whom we so easily place apart from us, are men and women just like you, with hopes and dreams. And they have children, just as precious to them as your children are to you. Our cheap stuff comes with a price tag: heartache and suffering.

Jesus wants to challenge our attitudes and behaviors toward things, because they affect our attitudes and behaviors toward people.

Mother Teresa wrote: "Live simply so that others may simply live." How many of the world's problems are caused because too often we love things and use people?

Money, Money, Money

Throughout the four Gospels, Jesus speaks about money more than any other topic. The reason, I suspect, is that nothing gets between us and God like money. Nothing will mess up our values and priorities like money.

Do you have a healthy relationship with money?

There are a thousand ways to have an unhealthy relationship with money. You can hoard it or waste it, use it to control others, or lust after more of it. The list goes on and on.

There is one way to have a healthy relationship with money: Remember it is not yours. Everything belongs to God. The money and things we have he has simply entrusted to us. We are stewards.

This realization gives birth to Gospel generosity. That's right, you guessed: Gospel generosity is radical.

Hungry to Be Noticed

Another hallmark of our culture is our inordinate desire to be noticed, to stand out, and our obsession with fame. Jesus was not interested in these things.

One of my favorite Bible passages is in the first chapter of Mark's Gospel. Jesus goes to a village and the people bring their family and friends asking him to heal them. He spends the evening healing the people. Early the next morning Simon comes looking for Jesus, who has gone off to a quiet place to pray, and says, "Everyone is looking for you." There would be a natural tendency for us to want to bathe in the glory of success, but Jesus basically says to Simon, "Let's get out of here" (see Mark 1:35–38).

The people of that village, and many before it and many after it, would have been more than happy to make Jesus their leader. They would have been more than happy to smother him with praise, status, riches, and every good thing this world has to offer. He rejected it all and moved on to the next place to fulfill his mission.

There Is No Place like Home

Consider the most basic element of our lifestyles. Where do you live? Where do you call home? Home is something most of us take for granted, but Jesus didn't have that. "Foxes have holes, and birds of the air have nests, but the Son of Man has nowhere to lay his head" (Luke 9:58).

It began, of course, with his radical entry into this world: a tiny ovum in the womb of an unmarried woman. Then there was the manger. He didn't have a reservation. The King of Kings and the Lord of Lords was born in a stable.

Throughout his entire public life, there is no record of Jesus going home. We read of him visiting the region where he was from, but there is nothing about him going back to his family home and certainly no record that he had a home of his own.

In all my years of travel, one of the most difficult things has been being away from home. There are a thousand things you take for granted at home—the feel of your own bed, the firmness of your pillows, the temperature and ability to control it, your preferred food and beverages in the refrigerator, and all your things. When you are on the road, you don't have any of this. Life on the road can make you feel unsettled, disoriented, unmoored.

When you have been away, whether for a few days or for many months, it is a wonderful feeling to come home. We yearn for home. The people of every nation and culture universally celebrate the feeling of arriving home, because it is a foreshadowing of our final journey home to be with God in heaven for eternity.

POINT TO PONDER: You need to work on your attitudes toward money, things, and people.

VERSE TO LIVE: "Do not store up for yourselves treasures on earth, where moth and rust consume and where thieves break in and steal; but store up for yourselves treasures in heaven." MATTHEW 6:19–20

QUESTION TO CONSIDER: What is one practical way you can live this teaching in the coming week?

PRAYER: Jesus, please rearrange my priorities. Help me to live a little bit more like you each day.

NINETEEN
Miracles Abound

YOU ARE SURROUNDED BY MIRACLES.

As we read the Gospels of Matthew, Mark, Luke, and John, we are constantly witnessing Jesus' miracles: turning water into wine, healing the sick, making the blind see, making the lame walk, casting out demons, feeding thousands with scraps, raising people from the dead, calming storms, walking on water, and making the deaf hear, to name but a few.

What are your favorite miracles of Jesus? If you could perform one of them, which would you choose? Why?

Ask a bunch of college kids and they will choose changing water into wine. But ask the mother of a chronically sick child and she will choose to heal her daughter.

Miracles are radical by their very nature, and so we shouldn't be surprised that they play a central role in Jesus' ministry. His miracles combined every aspect of his radical nature.

But in another sense, his miracles were ordinary. They were simple and practical, like his teachings. They were of real service to people, not just spectacular for the sake of being spectacular.

They required no great effort; they were simply an extension of who Jesus was. They were never performed for show or out of any ego need.

Making the lame walk, giving sight to the blind, setting captives free—these were all radical. Forgiving people's sins—even more radical. And these were just everyday aspects of Jesus' life.

It is easy to fall into the trap of placing these miracles in a far-off place with people you never knew. But they are also here and now. It's a miracle that he forgives our sins even though he knows we will sin again. Would you forgive someone if you knew he or she was going to do it again?

Part of Jesus' invitation is to bring the miracle of his love to others.

I have a friend who has had a very difficult life. A few years ago I noticed something that had been in front of me my whole life, but I had never connected the dots. Anytime we go to a social gathering of any type, he ends up spending the majority of his time at that event with the most unlikely person. When I became conscious of it, I asked him about it. He explained to me that he has suffered a lot in his life, and as a result, he can tell when someone else is suffering. I probed a little bit further, and this is what he said: "When I go into any room, I look for the person who is suffering the most, and I just try to ease their pain in whatever way I can."

I have seen this friend participate in everyday miracles with this one simple approach, which, it seems to me, comes straight out of the Gospel. But when most people walk into a room, they look for the people they will most enjoy speaking with, the people they want favors from, or whomever it is socially advantageous to be seen with.

Jesus didn't do this. Like my friend, it seems Jesus looked around the room and sought out the person most in pain or most in need.

The Gospels invite us to do small things with great love. Think of all the prayers people pray every day. Only a very small number of those prayers require God's direct involvement or intervention. Ordinary people like you and me can answer most prayers.

If we would just learn to recognize people's needs and pain, there are so many prayers that God wants to use us to answer. Too many go unanswered because ordinary people like you and me don't allow the Holy Spirit to guide us.

POINT TO PONDER: God wants to see your amazingness.

VERSE TO LIVE: "The one who believes in me will also do the works that I do, in fact, will do greater works than these." JOHN 14:12

QUESTION TO CONSIDER: Whose prayer can you be the answer to today?

PRAYER: Jesus, teach me to recognize the opportunity for everyday miracles.

TWENTY
Radical Love

LIFE IS A COURSE DESIGNED to teach us to love.

There are many different types of love. There is affection, which is a fondness developed through familiarity, most commonly found in families. There is friendship, such as the love that exists between girlfriends, or *mates*, as we would say in Australia. There is romantic love, the experience of being "in love" or loving someone in particular above all others. And there is agape, the unconditional love that Jesus models for us.

The way we respond to everything that happens in our lives causes us to either love more or love less. Sometimes we turn away from love because it can be painful. Sometimes we turn away from love because we don't want to be hurt. And sometimes we turn away from love because we are afraid of where it will lead us.

But wisdom lies in realizing that love is the only way. And yet, even once we realize this, it can still be a daily struggle to apply its wisdom to the events of our lives. It is not our natural inclination to love unconditionally, especially when we have been wronged.

This is where Jesus comes in. He came to teach us agape love, to teach us how to love without conditions.

The Gospels are the ultimate guide to agape love. This love is selfless, sacrificial, generous, and unconditional. By contrast, the types of love that are widely proclaimed and practiced in modern society are outrageously conditional. This creates a tremendous confusion about love.

Young people are obsessed with being liked, wanted, desired, and accepted, and they will do almost anything to obtain these. But deep down, what is it that they really want? Agape love. They want to be loved not because of how they look or what they can do for another person, but simply for who they are. That is how God loves us. Our yearning to be loved is a yearning for God.

And it's not just young people. This love confusion is now a multigenerational crisis. So many men and women are in long-standing relationships in which their acceptance is based on how they look or what they will do for the other person. They live in constant fear that if they stop looking a certain way or no longer please their partner they will be banished. These relationships give birth to all types of paranoia and neuroses. These are the fruits of control and manipulation, but not the fruits of love.

The love God wants to give you—and the love he wants you to give to others—is radically different. God loves you not because of anything you do for him. If you have children, you probably understand this love more now than before you had them. Parents love their children not because of what their children do, but simply because they are theirs. They get that instinct, that ability to love for love's sake, from God.

Love deeply desires everything that is good for the other person. This is why every day, in every country, regardless of culture or religion, parents make sacrifices for their children. They lay down their lives for the good of their children. This sacrificial love is inspiring. It is inspiring in a parent, and yet it fades in comparison to the outrageously generous sacrificial love that Jesus displayed by dying for us on the cross.

Dying on the cross was radical. Jesus was innocent and he could have escaped and avoided all the pain and suffering. The cross is radical love. "No one has greater love than this, to lay down one's life for one's friends" (John 15:13). Jesus poured himself out for us on the cross, but this was just the final expression of what he had been doing every day during his public life. He was constantly pouring himself out for others. Then he would go away to a quiet place to get reenergized so that he could pour himself out again.

Most radicals lead revolutions. There are economic revolutions and political revolutions. There are ideological revolutions and social revolutions. Many are violent and some are selfish. Often the leaders of revolutions have the most to gain. Most revolutions help some and hurt others. But Jesus' revolution helped everyone. His revolution is one of love, radical love.

We find the purest expression of that love in the cross. What's even more radical is that he invites us to love radically too. Let's resolve, right now, to love like we have never loved before.

Love is patient; love is kind; love is not envious or boastful or arrogant or rude. It does not insist on its own way; it is not irritable or resentful; it does not rejoice in wrongdoing, but rejoices in the truth. It bears all things, believes all things, hopes all things, endures all things. (1 Corinthians 13:4–8)

POINT TO PONDER: At the end, when you face God, perhaps what he will ask is: How well did you love?

VERSE TO LIVE: "Father, into your hands I commend my spirit." LUKE 23:46

QUESTION TO CONSIDER: What are you laying down your life for?

PRAYER: Jesus, teach me to love with abandon.

TWENTY-ONE

The Main Event

IT MUST HAVE BEEN SOME SUNDAY MORNING.

The most radical moment in the history of the world was that Sunday morning when Jesus rose from the dead. Ignore it if you wish or pretend it didn't happen, but it is simply impossible to make sense of life and history without acknowledging the Resurrection.

I think I could probably write a whole book about the Resurrection and not accomplish what Lee Strobel accomplished in the following short article:

"How Easter Killed My Faith in Atheism"

It was the worst news I could get as an atheist: my agnostic wife had decided to become a Christian. Two words shot through my mind. The first was an expletive; the second was "divorce."

I thought she was going to turn into a self-righteous holy roller. But over the following months, I was intrigued by the positive changes in her character and values. Finally, I decided to take my journalism and legal training (I was the legal editor of the *Chicago Tribune*) and systematically investigate whether there was any credibility to Christianity.

Maybe, I figured, I could extricate her from this cult.

I quickly determined that the alleged resurrection of Jesus was the key. Anyone can claim to be divine, but if Jesus backed up his claim by returning from the dead, then that was awfully good evidence he was telling the truth.

For nearly two years, I explored the minutiae of the historical data on whether Easter was a myth or reality. I didn't merely accept the New Testament at face value; I was determined only to consider facts that were well-supported historically. As my investigation unfolded, my atheism began to buckle.

Was Jesus really executed? In my opinion, the evidence is so strong that even atheist historian Gerd Ludermann said his death by crucifixion was "indisputable."

Was Jesus' tomb empty? Scholar William Lane Craig points out that its location was known to Christians and non-Christians alike. So if it hadn't been empty, it would have been impossible for a movement founded on the resurrection to have exploded into existence in the same city where Jesus had been publicly executed just a few weeks before.

Besides, even Jesus' opponents implicitly admitted the tomb was vacant by saying that his body had been stolen. But nobody had a motive for taking the body, especially the disciples. They wouldn't have been willing to die brutal martyrs' deaths if they knew this was all a lie.

Did anyone see Jesus alive again? I have identified at least eight ancient sources, both inside and outside the

New Testament, that in my view confirm the apostles' conviction that they encountered the resurrected Christ. Repeatedly, these sources stood strong when I tried to discredit them.

Could these encounters have been hallucinations? No way, experts told me. Hallucinations occur in individual brains, like dreams, yet, according to the Bible, Jesus appeared to groups of people on three different occasions—including 500 at once!

Was this some other sort of vision, perhaps prompted by the apostles' grief over their leader's execution? This wouldn't explain the dramatic conversion of Saul, an opponent of Christians, or James, the once-skeptical half-brother of Jesus.

Neither was primed for a vision, yet each saw the risen Jesus and later died proclaiming he had appeared to him. Besides, if these were visions, the body would still have been in the tomb.

Was the resurrection simply the recasting of ancient mythology, akin to the fanciful tales of Osiris or Mithras? If you want to see a historian laugh out loud, bring up that kind of pop-culture nonsense.

One by one, my objections evaporated. I read books by skeptics, but their counter-arguments crumbled under the weight of the historical data. No wonder atheists so often come up short in scholarly debates over the resurrection.

In the end, after I had thoroughly investigated the matter, I reached an unexpected conclusion: it would actually take more faith to maintain my atheism than to become a follower of Jesus.

And that's why I'm now celebrating my 30th Easter as a Christian. Not because of wishful thinking, the fear of death, or the need for a psychological crutch, but because of the facts.

Rising from the dead! Wow. The ultimate proof that Jesus was a radical is also the central premise of Christianity. This is the main event. Without the Resurrection Christianity is foolishness, Paul tells us (see 1 Corinthians 15:12–14).

Did the Resurrection of Jesus actually happen? Though there is plenty of evidence to suggest it to the open and honest heart, I cannot prove it. There has to be room for faith; otherwise it would be called certainty.

But if it did actually happen, if Jesus did rise from the dead, what else is left to be said?

POINT TO PONDER: God wants to resurrect you in some specific way.

VERSE TO LIVE: "You are looking for Jesus of Nazareth. . . . He is risen! He is not here." MARK 16:6

QUESTION TO CONSIDER: What area of your life needs resurrection right now?

PRAYER: Jesus, unleash the power of your resurrection. Resurrect the area of my life that most needs it today.

TWENTY-TWO
Beyond Tweaking

GOD HAS A MIGHTY, AWESOME, wonderful transformation in mind for you.

From time to time a debate emerges about why people don't read the Bible more. These discussions always give rise to a variety of reasons, which are then explored, discussed, and analyzed. Popular reasons include: People are intimidated by the various ancient texts, and people are simply too busy.

One of the reasons we don't read the Bible more is because we have become an increasingly impatient society. The Bible isn't like other books. It requires patience. It is like when you meet a fascinating person; it takes time to get to know him or her.

The more impatient we have become as a society, the more our relationships have suffered. Patience is at the core of any great relationship, because it takes patience to listen and really understand the heart of another person.

The Bible helps us know the heart of God and the heart of man. That takes time. It's not a self-help book, in which every line is filled with clichés and step-by-step directives. It is about learning God's heart and learning our own heart.

But in a deeply subconscious way, the explanation for why we don't read the Bible more is deeply profound: We *know* the Word of God has the power to transform our lives, and the uncomfortable, unspoken, and often-avoided truth is that we don't want our lives transformed. Be honest. Do you want God to completely overhaul your life and totally transform you?

Transformation may seem attractive in a moment of blissfully holy idealistic exuberance or at a moment of crisis, but the everyday reality is we like to distance ourselves from the inner work required to bring about such a transformation.

The long history of God's relationship with humanity has always displayed his preference for collaboration over intervention. God will not snap his fingers and bring about the type of transformation we are talking about here. He desires a dynamic collaboration with each of us. God wants us to do our part.

So, no, we don't necessarily want our lives transformed. Sure, we want some tweaking, but not transformation. This desire for tweaking is selective and selfish, while transformation is total and selfless.

Avoiding transformation has a very real impact on our spirituality. Once we abandon the transformation that is the Christian life, our focus falls on tweaking; our spirituality becomes mediocre and very self-centered. Then we start praying for tweaking: Dear God, please tweak this . . . and please tweak that . . . and tweak my spouse . . . and tweak my spouse again because it didn't take the first time . . . and tweak my kids . . . and tweak my boss . . . and tweak my colleagues at work . . . and tweak my son's soccer coach . . . and tweak my daughter's schoolteacher . . . and tweak our pastor . . . and tweak the politicians . . .

We pray for tweaking—and then we wonder why God doesn't answer our prayers. The reason is simple: God is not in the business of *tweaking*. He's in the business of *transformation*.

The other sad, tragic, miserable truth is that most of us have never prayed a prayer of transformation—not even once in our lives. Most of us have never come before God and prayed:

Loving Father,
Here I am.
I trust that you have an incredible plan for me.
Transform me. Transform my life.
Everything is on the table.
Take what you want to take and give what you want to give.
Transform me into the person you created me to be,
so I can live the life you envision for me.
I hold nothing back;
I am 100 percent available.
How can I help?
Amen.

If you want to see miracles, pray that prayer. If you want to see and experience miracles in your own life, pray a wholehearted prayer of transformation. That's a prayer God will answer. God always answers a prayer of transformation. Never once in the history of the world has God not answered a sincere prayer of transformation.

We need to start praying prayers that God can easily answer, prayers that God wants to answer. When we want what God wants, it becomes easy for him to answer our prayers. But too often we use prayer in a vain and futile attempt to impose our will upon God.

So what's it going to be: More tweaking or are you ready for transformation?

POINT TO PONDER: The butterfly emerges from the cocoon; it is a beautiful transformation.

VERSE TO LIVE: "So if anyone is in Christ, there is a new creation: everything old has passed away; see everything has become new!" 2 CORINTHIANS 5:17

QUESTION TO CONSIDER: What will be the hardest thing about letting God transform you and your life?

PRAYER: Jesus, keep the desire for transformation alive in my heart.

TWENTY-THREE

Upside Down

GOD WANTS TO TURN YOUR life upside down.

I might as well tell you now. We have been dancing all around it. Jesus wants to turn your life upside down—which, as it turns out, will be right side up. He wants to turn your marriage upside down, your parenting upside down, your personal finances upside down, your career upside down, your health and well-being upside down, your school and church upside down. If you let Jesus turn your life upside down, you will be happier than you ever imagined was possible. And you won't just have happiness—you will have joy!

This is what Jesus does. He radically transforms the lives of the people he encounters, by rearranging their priorities. Perhaps that is why we avoid a deeply personal encounter with Jesus, because we are afraid of that radical transformation. But you will look back a few years from now on things you thought were so very important today and realize that they were not—and that your new priorities have more truth, beauty, and wisdom.

Throughout the Gospels we see Jesus challenging people's priorities and in the process radically transforming their lives. Do you have a favorite story of transformation from the Gospels?

The story of Zacchaeus is a wonderful and radical tale of transformation. It's a very short story, but there are some beautiful lines. It begins by telling us who Zacchaeus was, and then it says, "He was trying to see who Jesus was." This tells us that he was proactively seeking Jesus. He was making an effort. He was curious. Zacchaeus climbed a tree to catch a glimpse of Jesus, and Jesus called him down from the tree and invited himself to dinner at Zacchaeus' house. We are then told, "So he hurried down and was happy to welcome him." There is no record of Jesus saying Zacchaeus should do this or that, or that he must change his life. Jesus' presence was apparently enough to transform Zacchaeus, who said to him, "Look, half of my possessions, Lord, I will give to the poor; and if I have defrauded anyone of anything, I will pay back four times as much." He didn't need anyone to tell him what he should do; his own heart prescribed the transformation that was needed (see Luke 19:1–10).

Are we proactively seeking Jesus? Are we making an effort to experience him? Are we curious about him? Are we in a hurry to meet him? Are we happy to welcome him? What change is your heart prescribing for your life?

The Gospels present a constant flow of people meeting Jesus. Each of them responded differently. Few responded with the unbridled enthusiasm of Zacchaeus. We could be tempted to think that the various responses were due to external circumstances, but it is more likely that the variety of responses is due to disposition of heart. We see this in the story of the ten lepers whom Jesus cured. They all encountered Jesus the healer, but only one returned with a grateful heart (see Luke 17:11–19).

Another obvious example of radical transformation is the call of the disciples. But there were others whose response to Jesus was much more gradual. Consider the story of Nicodemus. His is not limited to one passage of the Gospels, but rather evolves over time.

We first read of Nicodemus coming to Jesus in the night, presumably so that nobody would see him consulting Jesus. They conversed and then Nicodemus said, "How can these things be?" (John 3). For many people their first encounter with Jesus was enough to bring about a profession of faith and a radical transformation, but for others it was not. Nicodemus only had questions. People often have a deep yearning, a sense that there must be more to life, that there is some great truth that they have yet to discover. Perhaps this is what Nicodemus was experiencing when he first approached Jesus.

Later Nicodemus tried to defend Jesus by saying to the other Pharisees, "Does our law judge a man without first giving him a hearing and learning what he does?" (John 7:51).

Finally, we read of Nicodemus accompanying Joseph of Arimathea to ask Pilate for Jesus' body. He brought with him seventy-five pounds of aloe and myrrh. Together the two men took Jesus' body down from the cross, carried it to the tomb, and wrapped it with spices and linen for burial (see John 19:38–42).

One of the Christian works of mercy is to bury the dead. What Joseph and Nicodemus did here was one of the ultimate works of mercy in history. Nicodemus did all this at great personal risk to his reputation and safety. Think of the incredible courage this would have required.

What kept Nicodemus from a wholehearted embrace of Jesus? He was worried about what people thought—that is the most likely explanation for why he came to Jesus at night. He was a wise and learned man, but often it seems the uneducated came to Jesus more willingly than the educated. What we do know is that Nicodemus had a persistent desire to seek and find the truth. Only good things can come from continually seeking truth.

In each of these people who encountered Jesus, we find a piece of ourselves. Who cannot resonate in some way with the rich young man?

The rich young man proactively sought out Jesus. He didn't wait for Jesus to seek him out; he approached Jesus. He was clearly trying to live a good life. And it was not Jesus who was saying, "You can do more." The young man's own heart told him this. Finally Jesus said, "Go, sell what you own, and give the money to the poor ... then come, follow me" (Mark 10:21).

If Jesus asked you to do this today, could you?

When the young man heard this, "His face fell, and he went away sad, for he had many possessions" (Mark 10:22). This is the only time the word *sad* is used in the Gospels. When we turn from Jesus and walk away, it is always a sad walk.

I wonder what happened to that young man? Did he change his mind later? How long did it take for his heart to soften? Did he become one of the first Christians? There are so many questions that the Gospels raise. So many people wander into the story for a brief moment. We get just a glimpse of their lives; we never even learn the names of many of these people. But I find myself asking questions, wondering what happened to them. We don't know what happened to Nicodemus. Did he become a Christian? Did the woman Jesus saved from being stoned who had been caught in adultery "go and sin no more"?

Lazarus is another person I am fascinated with. Jesus raised him from the dead. What is it like to live on this side of death once you have experienced its other side? How did that change his worldview?

It reminds me of a story I once heard about twins in utero. One turns to the other and says, "I wonder if there is life after birth?" The reality of life on earth is astounding when compared to life in the womb, and I suspect that in the same way, the afterlife is astounding compared to life here on earth. So what was it like for Lazarus to come from that greater reality back to this lesser reality? Did he wish Jesus hadn't raised him from the dead? The Gospels are full of fascinating questions.

There were people who embraced Jesus immediately, there were people who were slow to embrace him, and there were people who rejected him. Pilate, for example, simply could not square Jesus with his worldview, because Pilate's worldview was dominated by power, ambition, control, and the things of this world. His worldview, and the heart it sprang forth from, made him simply incapable of accepting the reality of Jesus.

There were others who took a long time to come around. The centurion at the cross didn't realize who Jesus was until he died, when he proclaimed, 'Truly this was the Son of God" (Mark 15:39). In the Gospel of Mark, this was the first time a human being proclaimed that Jesus was the Son of God.

And the radically transformative encounters with Jesus did not cease when he died.

The most famous conversion story ever is that of Saul, the Christian-hating Jew who made it his personal mission to persecute and eradicate Christians. If it had been up to Saul, every Christian would have been dead or in prison, but that all changed on a trip to Damascus. "Now as he was going along and approaching Damascus" (Acts 9:3), we are told that Jesus appeared to Saul. He was forever transformed, changed his name to Paul, and became one of the most dedicated disciples of Jesus.

It must have been an incredible experience, because Paul would suffer tremendously for the rest of his life as a result of his belief in Jesus. The Jews tried to kill him because he publicly taught that Jesus was the Son of God, and he was imprisoned several times and spent years of his life deprived of liberty and dignity before being executed during Nero's persecution of Christians from 64 to 68 AD.

Paul's transformation was radical and wholehearted. For more than two thousand years Jesus has been radically transforming the lives of men, women, and children in every corner of the world. But that is history. Now he wants to radically transform you and your life. Are you ready?

Jesus was a radical, and he wants to have a radical impact on your life. The Gospel is a radical invitation to surrender and transformation. It was radical two thousand years ago, and it is still radical today.

Is it less radical to love your enemy today than it was two thousand years ago? Is it easier to love your enemy today than it was then? No. Why? Because these things are personal. They are about you. They are lessons that we each must learn to embrace and live for ourselves.

The Gospel has had a radical impact on countless lives since Jesus walked the earth, and it is guaranteed to have a radical impact on your life if you open yourself up to it.

POINT TO PONDER: Be open.

VERSE TO LIVE: "Create in me a clean heart, O God, and put a new and right spirit within me." PSALM 51:10

QUESTION TO CONSIDER: What's preventing you from making yourself available to God?

PRAYER: Jesus, I make myself 100 percent available to you today.

TWENTY-FOUR

The Gap

EVERYBODY HAS A GAP TO CLOSE.

At church on Sunday after the Gospel has been read I often ask myself: "If I just lived this one Gospel reading 100 percent, how much would my life change?" The answer is the same every Sunday: radically. My life would change radically if I just lived one parable or teaching from any of the four Gospels 100 percent.

What that tells me is that there is a gap between my life and the Gospel. And it's a big gap. It's an obvious gap. It's not even a close call. There is a gaping hole between my life and the life Jesus invites me to live in the Gospel.

It's good to recognize the gap. Part of the problem, it seems, is that most of us think we are pretty good Christians. But compared to what? If we compare ourselves to what we see in the movies, sure, many of us might almost be considered saints. But is that a true measure of a Christian? I don't think so. Perhaps you look around you and see a friend who is an alcoholic and a negligent father, another who is addicted to pornography, and another who is involved in an adulterous affair with her next-door neighbor. Maybe compared to them you are an excellent Christian.

But when the young man came to Jesus and said, "Teacher, what must I do to inherit eternal life?" (Luke 18:18). Jesus didn't say, "Oh, just be better than the people around you."

Everyone can find a comparison to make them feel good about themselves. This charade assists us in deceiving ourselves in a thousand ways. This is the sin of comparison.

Some people may look at the gap between the life I am currently leading and the Gospel and judge me. They may be tempted to think, "He says he is a Christian, but he does this or that." They may be tempted to say, "He is a hypocrite." They would be right. I have no defense. I struggle every day to live the life Jesus invites us to. I am weak and broken. I have biases and prejudices. I am a sinner. But knowing I am a sinner is not the same as self-loathing. So I will not give up. I will press on, trying to be better and do better.

Despite this gap, I still consider myself a disciple of Jesus. Being Christian is not about being perfect. Membership among the followers of Jesus Christ does not require perfection. But it does require us to strive to live as Jesus invites us to live. And that means working diligently to close the gap.

I say diligently because being Christian requires proactive intentionality. It doesn't just happen. It requires us to actively seek out God and his will in the situations of daily life, and to work each day to close the gap between the person we are and the person he created us to be. It is striving to be the-very-best-version-of-ourselves, and it animates us.

So how do we work on closing the gap? We do it by getting close to Jesus.

Throughout Jesus' life we witness one person after another clamoring to get close to him. To the people of his time, it was obvious that he had special powers and that simply being close to him could be of tremendous benefit. As a result, wherever he was, people crowded around him. If he was teaching in the synagogue, walking down the road, or eating in someone's home, people went out of their way to get close to him.

One of the most powerful examples of this in the Scriptures is the woman who had been suffering for twelve years with an illness, who says, "If I can just touch his cloak I will be made well" (Matthew 9:21).When was the last time you went out of your way to get close to Jesus?

Two thousand years of Christianity and yet the wisdom of living out the Gospel in any age is unchanged: Get close to Jesus and stay close to him.

If you want to stay warm, it is best to stay close to the fire. If you want to live a Christian life, it is best to stay close to Jesus.

•●◆●•

There are so many ways to get close to Jesus. Some are simple and can be practiced in the flow of our everyday activity, while others require a time and a place set apart from this busy, noisy world. But they all require effort.

At the beginning of our time together, I promised you a simple starting point. Over the next four sections, I am going to outline four practical ways to get close to Jesus, stay close to him, and close the gap. There are a hundred ways to rediscover Jesus, but I chose these four because I knew even the busiest person could do them. This is a path for busy people.

So allow me to set before you four practical daily ways to rediscover Jesus:

1. **Read the four Gospels**, over and over again, for fifteen minutes each day.

2. **Practice The Prayer Process**. This is a simple process designed to help you enter into a daily conversation with Jesus.

3. **Deny yourself**. Find a handful of small ways to deny yourself each day.

4. **Practice spontaneous prayer**. Talk to Jesus about the events of your day as they are unfolding.

How would you like your life to change? What aspects of your life are you discontent with? At different times we all want our lives to change. How would you like your life to be different one year from now?

Our lives change when our habits change. God uses new habits to transform us. These four habits will have a beautiful and radical impact on your life if you allow them to sink their roots deep into your life.

So, begin now. This is a fresh start. Be bold. Embrace it with the enthusiasm of a child. Resist any temptation to put it off. Close the gap.

Begin it now.

POINT TO PONDER: Do not be afraid of what God is inviting you to right now.

VERSE TO LIVE: "I am confident of this, that the one who began a good work in you will bring it to completion." PHILIPPIANS 1:6

QUESTION TO CONSIDER: Why do you resist the happiness that God wants to fill you with?

PRAYER: Jesus, give me the courage to begin and the courage to continue.

TWENTY-FIVE

Delve into the Gospels

FIND YOURSELF IN THE GOSPELS.

When I was about fifteen years old, my spiritual mentor gave me an old Bible and encouraged me to read the Gospels. I had heard stories read at church each week, but I had never read the Gospels, not even one of them, from start to finish.

It changed my life. I realized that Jesus is not just a historic figure. He is alive and with us in everything we do.

At the time, I didn't know that the man who had given me the Bible was becoming my spiritual mentor. I thought it was just another isolated event in my life. But I will always be so grateful that he put that worn Bible in my hands and gave me a starting point.

If he had not given me that starting point, if he had not said, "Begin with the Gospels," who knows what would have happened? I probably would have begun with Genesis—and then who knows if I would be writing this book today?

As children we are given all sorts of vaccinations to protect us from a variety of diseases. But how does a vaccine work? It contains a little of the disease itself. By receiving a tiny portion of the disease, your body learns to fight it off. Through this process you become inoculated. Once you are inoculated you become immune to that particular disease.

Most Christians have been inoculated against the Gospel. They have been given a "vaccine" that contains a small-enough dose of Christianity that they have become immune to the Gospel. Somewhere along the way they were given a little bit of Christianity, and now they think they know all about it. Millions who have rejected Christianity have no idea what they have rejected. Many Christians have been inoculated against Christianity. They may go to church on Sunday and in many ways be good members of society, but the inoculation prevents them from truly embracing the Christian faith.

It is impossible to rediscover Jesus without rediscovering the Gospels. The Gospels are a starting point, a primary source of rediscovery.

I have said it before, and I will say it again: Read the Gospels for fifteen minutes a day, every day. Allow the life and teachings of Jesus to sink their roots deep into your life. This will help you to get beyond your vague familiarity with the Gospels and develop a living, breathing, practical intimacy with them. If you make reading and reflecting on the Gospels a habit in your life, in time it will become a touchstone of inspiration and solace.

To begin, find a place where you can be still and quiet. Decide a time each day that is set apart just for this. Develop a routine for this daily habit, allowing it to become an immovable part of each day. Together with the other three habits, this will begin to create a powerful rhythm to your days.

You may ask, "Won't I get bored reading the Gospels over and over again?" Not if you approach them in a new way each time. There are a thousand ways to read the life of Jesus Christ, and how we read it determines the experience we have.

Where are you when you read the Gospels? Are you here and now, in modern-day America, two thousand years later, looking way back into the past? That's one way, but I'd suggest you imagine yourself there in the scene while it is unfolding before you and around you!

Remember the story about the paralytic whose friends lowered him through the roof so that Jesus could heal him? Imagine yourself there. Who are you? One of the houseguests? One of the paralytic's friends bringing him to Jesus to be healed? What great friends! Or are you the paralytic, having a life-changing encounter with Jesus?

Our tendency is to approach the Gospels as history, far removed from who and where we are today. The temptation is to distance ourselves and approach them in an impersonal way. But the Gospels are a living, breathing, deeply personal experience. If we are to encounter the living Jesus as powerfully as possible, we need to learn to place ourselves there, in each scene, seeing, hearing, smelling, and tasting everything that is happening, contemplating what each person in the scene is thinking, feeling, hoping, fearing.

There are an infinite number of fresh ways to approach reading the Gospels. Sometimes I like to read with a theme in mind. For example, I might read Matthew's Gospel using generosity as a lens to look deeper into the people and events. Which people are generous? Which are not? Why? Patience, courage, compassion, awareness, spiritual and emotional blindness, humility, and pride—these are just a few of the many themes to explore the Gospels anew.

If you want to rediscover Jesus, the first step is to delve into the Gospels. They are the most comprehensive record of who Jesus was when he walked the earth, what he did, how he lived, and what he taught.

The Scriptures play a powerful role in the life of a Christian. The Word of God equips us for the mission God wants to send us on. Timothy teaches us, "All scripture is inspired by God and is useful for teaching, for reproof, for correction, and for training in righteousness, so that everyone who belongs to God may be proficient, equipped for every good work" (2 Timothy 3:16).

The four Gospels provide incredible insights into who Jesus was and who he is inviting you to become.

POINT TO PONDER: Jesus' teachings are astoundingly practical when we pause to reflect on them.

VERSE TO LIVE: "Your word is a lamp to my feet and a light to my path." PSALM 119:105

QUESTION TO CONSIDER: Have you ever really read the Gospels?

PRAYER: Jesus, reveal yourself to me as I begin to rediscover you through the Gospels.

TWENTY-SIX
The Prayer Process

PRAYER CHANGES EVERYTHING.

It is impossible to get close to Jesus and stay close to him without developing an intimate daily conversation with him. This conversation has two main parts: scheduled prayer and spontaneous prayer.

Each day we need a time that is set aside exclusively for prayer. This focused time of prayer each day, when we step away from the world to speak with God, is indispensable. We simply cannot grow spiritually without a consistent and persistent effort to pray; the Christian life is simply not sustainable without it.

There are two problems that prevent us from developing this habit of daily prayer. The first is that most Christians have never been taught how to pray. The second is that when people do make a sincere effort to pray, they don't know where to start or finish or what to do, so they tend to sit down and just see what happens. Of course, most of the time when we sit down in prayer and just see what happens, nothing happens. This becomes very discouraging, and as a result most people stop praying.

The Prayer Process was developed to give people a format for their daily prayer experience. It has a starting point and an ending point. It is a simple way to focus our prayer time. When we become distracted—and distraction is an inevitable part of prayer— we have a place to return to rather than allowing our distraction to end our prayer.

More than anything else, The Prayer Process is designed to facilitate an intimate conversation with God about not only the things that are happening in your life but also the things that are happening deep in your heart and soul—and to discern God's will for our lives.

Prayer is not the place for trivial conversation that avoids all the real issues. It is the place to get into everything that brings us high and low, to explore our hopes and dreams, our fears and concerns, our light and our dark sides and deepest desires. Prayer is not the place to hold back.

Perhaps what I like most about The Prayer Process is that it grows as we grow. It can be used as a starting point for beginners, those first trying to forge the habit of prayer in their lives. But it can also be used by those most advanced in their spiritual life. Its structure is such that it celebrates where you are in the journey.

The Prayer Process

1. **Gratitude:** Begin by thanking God in a personal dialogue for whatever you are most grateful for today.

2. **Awareness:** Revisit the times in the past twenty-four hours when you were and were not the-best-version-of-yourself.

Talk to God about these situations and what you learned from them.

3. **Significant Moments:** Identify something you experienced today and explore what God might be trying to say to you through that event (or person).

4. **Peace:** Ask God to forgive you for any wrong you have committed (against yourself, another person, or him) and to fill you with a deep and abiding peace.

5. **Freedom:** Speak with God about how he is inviting you to change your life, so that you can experience the freedom to be the-best-version-of-yourself.

6. **Others:** Lift up to God anyone you feel called to pray for today, asking God to bless and guide them.

7. Finish by praying the **Our Father**.

Nothing compares to establishing the habit of regular prayer in our lives. It is one of life's quintessential experiences.

What would your life be like if you prayed using The Prayer Process every day for a month? Would you have more joy? Would you be better at making decisions? Would you be clearer about what matters most and what matters least? Would you be better at saying no?

The habit of daily prayer will transform you in unimaginable ways, and you will wonder how you ever lived without it. We can survive without prayer, but we cannot thrive without it.

Are you thriving or just surviving?

POINT TO PONDER: God yearns to spend time with you each day in prayer.

VERSE TO LIVE: In the morning, while it was still very dark, he got up and went out to a deserted place, and there he prayed." MARK 1:35

QUESTION TO CONSIDER: Are you making spiritual progress?

PRAYER: Jesus, fill me with the grace to set aside a few minutes each day to spend just chatting with you.

TWENTY-SEVEN

Deny Yourself

LEARNING TO DELAY GRATIFICATION IS ONE of life's essential lessons.

Our ability to succeed at most things in life can be measured by our ability and willingness to delay gratification. You cannot have a successful marriage, be a great parent, maintain good health, establish financial stability, or become educated unless you are willing to delay gratification. The best at anything are better than everyone else at delaying gratification—and that includes the great Christian heroes, champions, and saints who fill the history books.

You cannot be successful at living a Christian life if you are not willing and able to practice self-denial. So, how good are you at it? Give yourself a score right now, between one and ten, for your ability to delay gratification.

Change that score and you change everything: You become more patient with your spouse and children, you work out more regularly instead of blowing it off, you get better at saying no to snacks you don't need, your personal finances improve because you establish and stick to a budget . . . the benefits go on and on. This is the beautiful thing about Jesus' teachings. They reach into every aspect of our lives and elevate everything.

We are on a quest to rediscover Jesus. It is a lifetime quest, and these four habits will serve us well every day for the rest of our lives if we stick with them.

The third habit that will help us get and stay close to Jesus is self-denial. For two thousand years Christians have been agreeing and disagreeing about what it means to be a Christian, debating and arguing various topics and points. But some things are indisputably essential to being a Christian, and self-denial is one of them.

Jesus said to his disciples, "If anyone wishes to come after me, he must deny himself and take up his cross daily and follow me" (Luke 9:23). Self-denial has an incredible impact on a human being. It refines the soul, sharpens the senses, strengthens the will, and tempers our desires.

We will explore this more in a later section, but let me offer this starting point: Say no to yourself at least once a day. Perhaps you are craving a Coke. Say no and have water. Perhaps you don't want to exercise. Say no to your laziness and work out. Perhaps you don't feel like getting on with your work. Get on with it.

Your life will be infinitely better if you learn to deny yourself. Just say no.

POINT TO PONDER: Learning to deny yourself will pay huge dividends in your life.

VERSE TO LIVE: "But the fruit of the Spirit is love, joy, peace, patience, kindness, generosity, faithfulness, gentleness, and self-control." GALATIANS 5:22–23

QUESTION TO CONSIDER: In what area of your life do you exhibit the most self-control? In what area of your life do you exhibit the least self-control?

PRAYER: Jesus, give me the grace and the strength to say no to myself.

TWENTY-EIGHT
Spontaneous Prayer

GOD DELIGHTS IN CONVERSATION WITH YOU.

We spoke already about a time dedicated to prayer each day. The second aspect of our daily conversation with God is the spontaneous turning to him during moments of the day to thank him, to ask him for help, guidance, encouragement, or simply to recognize him at our side.

This second type of conversation tends to spring forth from the first, more focused time set apart for prayer. There are some people who will say, "I don't have a set time of prayer each day, but I am constantly speaking with God throughout the day." It has been my experience that these people are deceiving themselves in a number of ways, and making little if any spiritual progress.

The daily casual conversation with God tends to be kept alive by the focused time of prayer each day. When we neglect our daily prayer time, the casual conversation becomes less frequent. If we neglect our daily time of prayer for long enough, the casual conversation throughout the day will die out almost entirely, the exception being those astounding moments in life that force us

to our knees. The richness of our spontaneous conversation with God flows from having a time set aside exclusively for prayer each day. This spontaneous prayer can become one of the great joys and comforts of the Christian life.

The first Christian prayers provide fabulous insight into how to develop a rich spontaneous prayer life. In the opening chapters of the Acts of the Apostles, we read about the first Christians. But I am not speaking here of the prayers of the first Christians, but rather the first Christian prayers.

It would seem to me that the first Christian prayers are the words that the various characters in the Gospels spoke directly to Jesus. They provide a prayer for every occasion in life. And perhaps every prayer that has been uttered ever since is just a variation of one of these first Christian prayers. Let's take a look at some.

One of my favorites is the second prayer of the blind man Bartimaeus. Hearing that Jesus was passing by, he began to cry out, "Jesus, Son of David, have mercy on me!" This cry for mercy was his first prayer. The crowd told him to be quiet, but he cried out all the more and all the louder: "Jesus, Son of David, have mercy on me!" Here Bartimaeus is teaching us one of the fundamentals of prayer: persistence. Finally, Jesus summoned the blind man and said to him, "What do you want me to do for you?" Bartimaeus replied, "Lord, open my eyes, so that I may see." This was his second prayer (see Mark 10:46–52).

I think I have probably prayed this prayer a million times in my life. "Lord, open my eyes, so that I may see." I pray this one all the time, over and over, a hundred times a day when I am trying to make a decision and I need light, guidance, and wisdom. These first Christian prayers are both fascinating and immensely practical.

There are two great professions of faith in the Gospels: Peter's and Thomas'. Each is a prayer unto itself. We have already spoken of Peter's profession of faith in the region of Caesarea Philippi, where he declared in answer to the Jesus question: "You are the Messiah, the Son of the living God" (Matthew 16:15). Now let's explore it from another angle. When was the last time you consciously acknowledged that Jesus is the Messiah? When was the last time you said it? When was the last time you said it out loud? When was the last time you said it to Jesus? We all need to profess our faith in Jesus regularly to keep things in perspective.

The other great profession of faith is that of Thomas. Absent the first time Jesus appeared to the disciples, Thomas became the great doubter. When Jesus appeared to them the second time, Thomas professed in awe, "My Lord and my God" (John 20:28).

This phrase has also played a rich part in my faith journey. In the church of my childhood, there was a small banner behind the altar with MY LORD AND MY GOD embroidered on it. I saw it every Sunday. It's a small thing. But those words became engraved first in my mind and then in my heart.

There are hundreds of these first Christian prayers as you make your way through the Gospels. The leper said to Jesus, "Lord, if you choose, you can make me clean" (Matthew 8:2). The centurion asked Jesus to cure his servant: "Lord, I am not worthy that you enter under my roof, but only say the word and my servant will be healed" (Matthew 8:8). During a storm out on a boat the disciples turned to Jesus and said, "Lord, save us! We are perishing!" (Matthew 8: 25).

In the prelude to the feeding of the five thousand, the disciples said to Jesus, "We have nothing here but five loaves and two fish." How often we come to Jesus in the same way, having so very little to offer to a situation. But just as Jesus said to the disciples, he says to us, "Bring me what you have" (Matthew 14:17). Jesus can work miracles with the little we have, if we bring it to him.

Peter teaches us another great lesson through his humanity in the scene in which Jesus came walking to them on the water. Jesus beckoned Peter to walk out onto the water, which he did. But Peter became distracted and took his eyes off Jesus. He became frightened, crying out, "Lord save me!" (Matthew 14:30).

In the same way, when we take our eyes off Jesus we begin to sink. And yet, often when we are sinking, we don't have the wisdom to cry out, "Lord save me!"

Many of these first prayers directed at Jesus were dripping with humanity. A perfect example is Martha complaining to Jesus, "Lord, do you not care that my sister has left me to do all the work by myself?" (Luke 10:40). Do you complain to God?

Even Jesus' mother contributes to the litany of first Christian prayers. These are the only recorded words we have of Mary speaking to Jesus: "They have no wine" (John 2:3). The way she spoke to Jesus is different from the way everyone else spoke to him. Her words are casual, practical, matter-of-fact, and they declare a familiarity that others did not have with Jesus.

There are also prayers in the Gospels that I hope I never have to pray. A man came to him, knelt before him, and said, "Lord, have mercy on my son" (Matthew 17:14). He knelt. He was begging. I hope to never have to beg God in this way for my children, but I suspect in different ways for different reasons, every parent begs God for their children.

This father's prayer was physical and verbal. He didn't just speak to Jesus; he knelt before him. When was the last time you knelt down to pray? It may seem old-fashioned, but when was the last time you knelt beside your bed at night and prayed? It's a powerful experience. Try it one night this week: Kneel beside your bed before you go to sleep, and pray. Pray aloud and it will be even more powerful.

Throughout the Gospels we also encounter phenomenal displays of faith, in many cases from the people we would least expect them from. Who can forget the Canaanite woman who came to Jesus seeking healing for her daughter and got into a back-and-forth banter with the Son of God? Finally, she won Jesus over with the line, "Yes, Lord, yet even the dogs eat the crumbs that fall from their master's table" (Matthew 15:27). Hers was a bold and beautiful faith.

There are also the simple yet profound prayers of gratitude, like Peter's just before the Transfiguration: "Lord, it is good for us to be here" (Matthew 17:4).

Some of these first Christian prayers were prophetic. Take, for example, Peter saying to Jesus, "Even though I must die with you, I will not deny you" (Matthew 26:35). It was a holy prayer coming from a good place in Peter's heart. He wasn't able to live up to it at the time, but ultimately he did, by dying for his faith when he was crucified under Nero. He requested that he be crucified upside down, as he believed he was unworthy to be crucified in the same way as Jesus.

There are the unforgettable moments, such as when the thief turned to Jesus and said, "Jesus, remember me when you come into your kingdom" (Luke 23:42). Do you think much about Jesus' kingdom? Is it part of your reality? Or has your view of realty shrunken to exclude it?

Of course, not every word spoken to Christ was respectful and reverent. But we can learn from every single word that was uttered by any person in the Gospels.

The mother of the sons of Zebedee came to Jesus to ask for a favor: "Declare that these two sons of mine will sit, one at your right hand and one at your left, in your kingdom." This was a selfish prayer. We have all prayed selfish prayers. We have all come to ask God for favors, sometimes for good reasons and other times for vain or selfish reasons. Every time we bring a petition to Jesus, we should ask ourselves: What is my motive in asking for this? (See Matthew 20:20 and John 21:18–19.)

To approach Jesus selfishly is one thing; to approach him disrespectfully is another. There were many who disrespected Jesus, including the Pharisees, who were cynical and skeptical, and disrespectful to Jesus. We all know people today who approach Jesus in the same way, or refuse to approach him.

In preparing to write this book, I tried to take a fresh look at the Gospels and all the people in them. I was hoping to rediscover Jesus by rediscovering the people he interacted with. The thing that fascinated me about the Pharisees as I rediscovered them was that they were always accusing Jesus of blasphemy. This was their big hang-up when it came to Jesus. To blaspheme is to speak of God in an irreverent, impious manner. The paradox is that the Pharisees were in fact the ones blaspheming, in the way they spoke to Jesus and about him.

There were others who even mocked Jesus. "The soldiers mocked him, 'Hail King of the Jews!' and spat at him" (Matthew 27:29). Can you imagine mocking God? We see it more and more in movies and television shows, just as we increasingly hear people taking the Lord's name in vain. It has become alarmingly common in our culture today, both in entertainment and in everyday life. It seems like four guys cannot play a round of golf without someone taking the Lord's name in vain.

Let me ask you this: Which of the Ten Commandments is the easiest to live? The second commandment is exclusively dedicated to the name of God: "You shall not take the name of the Lord your God in vain." A whole commandment is set aside just for God's name. That tells us speech is powerful—obviously much more so than we realize. I think this commandment is probably the easiest to keep. And if we so blatantly struggle as a culture to live the easiest of the commandments, what does that tell us about our spiritual state?

•◦●◦•

Throughout the Gospels people call out to Jesus in a variety of ways, and each is a prayer of one sort or another. There are hundreds of these first Christian prayers. As you read the Gospels, take note of them. Pause to consider each. Ask yourself: Have I ever spoken to Jesus like this? Have I ever prayed like this? These first Christian prayers are another wonderful theme to explore as we read the Gospels.

Learn to call out to God in the moments of your day, casually, in a very human way—like a small child speaks to her father.

Our best days are those when we stay connected with God throughout the day.

POINT TO PONDER: God is always at my side to help me make the best decisions.

VERSE TO LIVE: "Rejoice always, pray constantly, give thanks in all circumstances." 1 THESSALONIANS 5:16–18

QUESTION TO CONSIDER: What are you most grateful for today?

PRAYER: Jesus, thank you for being at my side even when I forget you are there.

TWENTY-NINE
Dancing for Joy

GOD WANTS TO TEACH YOU TO DANCE.

What I am proposing is not going to be easy. If it were easy it would be common. And yet, among the more than two billion Christians on the planet today, there are very few who take their faith seriously and approach it with the rigor of a champion.

In every age there is much talk about the state of the world, and our times are no different. The world is a mess. We experience this mess in a hundred ways every day. There is a lot of talk about changing the world, but even the idea of changing the world has become cliché. Most people today don't actually believe the world can be changed. But it can.

How? The change will not come from governments. They have their role, but you cannot legislate goodness, virtue, and morality. These things come only from a heart open to God. The change will not come from the economy and big business. They also have their role, but there is no evidence that more money or a better standard of living leads to a better world in the ways that matter most. The change will not come from science, for its role is primarily a passive one of observation.

There is no group of people in a better position to change the world than Christians. In fact, I think it can be argued that if Christians don't change the world, the world will not change.

So, how will we change the world? The answer is simple but not easy.

We will change the world simply by behaving like Christians. There are two billion Christians on the planet—anything we do together will have enormous influence. If Christians simply behaved as Christians, the world would be a different place in a matter of weeks.

But we have all failed to bring the message we receive at church on Sunday into every corner of our lives and society. And when we fail to live as we have been powerfully invited to live by Jesus in the Gospels, the incredible joy of God begins to leak from our lives.

There are two beautiful passages worth reflecting on here. The first is in 2 Samuel 6, when David was bringing the Ark of the Covenant toward Jerusalem. We read about these scenes in which David was shouting for joy—leaping and dancing for joy—before the Ark.

What did the Ark of the Covenant represent? For the Jewish people it represented the presence of God. They carried the Ark around reverently for forty years in the desert to remind themselves that God was with them. So David was shouting for joy, leaping for joy, dancing for joy in the presence of God.

The second passage is the Visitation, in Luke 1. Here we read about Elizabeth's unborn child, John the Baptist, dancing for joy in his mother's womb when he heard Mary's greeting. Of course, Mary was also pregnant, carrying the child Jesus. This makes Mary the Ark of the New Covenant.

Why was John the Baptist leaping for joy? For the same reason David danced for joy: because he was in the presence of God.

Living in the presence of God causes us to dance for joy. It is easy to lose sight of his presence. It is easy to wander from his ways. It is easy to become blind to his presence as a result of the crippling selfishness that we all fall victim to if we are left to our own devices. Fortunately, God is not content leaving us to our own devices.

The presence of Jesus is powerful. When he was walking the earth his presence demanded a response. Many people loved him, and some people hated him. But very few were indifferent to him. Jesus swayed people. His powerful presence moved them. It challenged them to choose good or evil. His presence was calming at times, and tempestuous at times. His presence ignited the full range of human emotions in the people following him.

But imagine the joy of being close. Imagine the joy Mary and Joseph had watching Jesus play as a child. Imagine the joy of walking down a dusty road with him, listening to his parables or just marveling at his presence as the group walked along quietly. Imagine the joy of having Jesus come to your home for dinner, the joy of introducing your family and friends to him.

The more we close the gap between the person we are today and the person God created us to be, the more we will experience that joy. The more we close the gap between the life we are living today and the life Jesus invites us to live through the Gospels, the more we will experience that joy.

So what stops us from closing the gap and dancing for joy?

POINT TO PONDER: There is nothing like the joy that God wants to fill your heart with.

VERSE TO LIVE: "A joyful heart is good medicine."
PROVERBS 17:22

QUESTION TO CONSIDER: Who or what is robbing you of joy?

PRAYER: Lord, teach me to dance for joy.

THIRTY
Blind Spots

WE ALL HAVE BLIND SPOTS.

There is one fundamental truth that we each need to come to grips with if we want to grow spiritually. Unless we are willing to embrace this truth, any spiritual growth we do experience will be stilted, minimal, and not a fraction of what is actually possible. It may be the first truth of the spiritual life. It is a truth that we need to be constantly reminded of. Others can and will remind us of this truth, but as we grow in wisdom we learn to remind ourselves.

This is the truth: We don't see things as they really are—especially ourselves. We all think we have twenty-twenty vision in life, but we don't. We don't see things as they really are.

Let me give you an example. Do you play golf? If you do, you will understand this example. (If you don't, think about a time you watched a recording of yourself.) Have you ever had your golf swing recorded? When you got the recording back, did your swing look like what you thought it would? Probably not. How many surprises were there? Probably not just one tiny one. You most likely didn't watch the recording and think, "The only problem is I take the club a fraction outside the line on the way back; other than that, my golf swing is perfect." No. If you examine it, really study it, you will see that you could probably improve your grip, your stance, where the ball sits in your setup, your tempo, your release at the top, the follow-through, and many other things. In your mind you may have thought you had a nice, easy swing like Fred Couples', but the recording doesn't lie and it quickly dispels that myth.

We don't see things as they really are. If you think this is not true, record yourself doing anything. You don't look like what you think you look like. You don't move like you think you move. You don't sound like what you think you sound like. Here's another example: Get out some old photos, from perhaps twenty years ago. Did you think you looked like that at the time?

We don't see things as they really are. You don't see your *marriage* as it really is. You don't see your *parenting* as it really is. You don't see your *career* as it really is. You don't see your *personal finances* as they really are. You don't see your *health* as it really is. You don't see your *business* as it really is. You don't see your *children's school* as it really is. You don't see your *church* as it really is. You don't see your life as it really is.

If you want to have a mind-altering experience, get four or five of your close friends together and ask them to tell you about how they see your marriage or your parenting. See if your friendship can survive that.

For more than twenty years, I have had various spiritual directors, people to coach me spiritually. They have helped me to grapple with the questions of life. They have listened to me dream and complain. They have helped me discern what God was calling me to next. But perhaps most of all they have helped me to catch glimpses of myself as I really am. Not as I imagine myself to be, not how I pretend to be, but as I really am. Not as I hope people will experience me, but as people actually experience me.

When I come to my spiritual coach and share something I am struggling with, half the time I need him to say, "Matthew, you're being too hard on yourself." The other half of the time, I need him to say, "Matthew, you're being too easy on yourself." And occasionally I need him to say, "You really need to pay attention to this, because it could become a real problem."

In the same way, sometimes I need my wife, Meggie, to take me aside and say, "Matthew, you're working too much," or "Matthew, you were too hard on Walter today; you need to remember he is only five years old."

I don't see things as they really are. I don't see myself as I really am. The reason is because I have blind spots. My past is full of experiences that are influencing my present and my future. These past experiences have given birth to fear and insecurity, which create huge blind spots. The past has also given birth to a thousand hopes, dreams, and ambitions that I carry deep within me, and these also prevent me from seeing myself as I really am. At times I can be cynical because of something or someone I encountered in the past, and this cynicism is a blind spot. I can also be paranoid at times—another blind spot. And guess what—I like being liked, and nothing will blind us like our desire to be liked, accepted, loved.

All of these blind spots make it hard for me to see situations and people (especially myself) as they really are. And if you are honest with yourself, I think you will discover you have blind spots too. Once we recognize and accept this, the real work can begin, because three things happen. We develop humility; we become docile to the promptings of the Holy Spirit, and we stop judging ourselves and other people.

Humility. Only the humble soul can be led. Only the humble soul is coachable. Only the humble soul can truly advance in the spiritual life.

Pride fuels the delusion that we see ourselves as we really are and situations for what they really are. It blinds us to who we really are. Pride prevents us from allowing God to transform us radically. Pride stops us from experiencing the fullness of joy that God desires for us.

Docility. God sends the Holy Spirit to guide us. In every moment of every day, the Holy Spirit is prompting us to do this or avoid that, to help this person or encourage another person. But in order to benefit from the promptings of the Holy Spirit in the moments of the day, we need to be docile.

What does it mean to be docile? It means to listen deeply and to be coachable. How well do you listen to the voice of God in the moments of the day, especially in times of decision? Are you stuck in your ways, or are you open to being coached in new and better ways?

Once we accept that we do not see ourselves and situations as they really are, we become humble, and one of the hallmarks of humility is docility.

Judging. There are so many ways to judge other people, and to judge ourselves. When we judge we pretend to be God. This is the grandest delusion in history: man thinking that he is God.

Opinions are a highly evolved way of judging. And we have opinions on everything. We live in a hyper-opinionated society, which is also to say we live in a hyper-judgmental society. In many ways, our opinions are a subtle, self-justified way of judging other people.

Judging emerges from pride. Opinions are an easy trap for the proud. Are you a judgmental person? Do you offer opinions without being asked? Do you offer opinions about things that you know little about? Do your opinions lead you and others closer to God?

∙•◆•∙

We all have a distorted view of reality. We don't see things as they really are; we don't see ourselves as we really are. We have blind spots, biases, and prejudices. Jesus wants to liberate us from all of these and help us to see things as they really are, to see ourselves as we really are.

POINT TO PONDER: We all have blind spots.

VERSE TO LIVE: "Why do you see the speck in your neighbor's eye, but do not notice the log in your own eye?" MATTHEW 7:3

QUESTION TO CONSIDER: How are your blind spots affecting your relationships?

PRAYER: Lord, take the blindness from my eyes so that I can see people, situations, and myself as you do.

THIRTY-ONE

Man's Ways and God's Ways

GOD HAS A BETTER WAY OF DOING THINGS.

Once we accept that we have a distorted view of reality, something can be done about it. Throughout the Scriptures we are taught that God's ways are not man's ways. In Isaiah we read: "Your thoughts are not my thoughts, nor are your ways my ways, declares the Lord" (Isaiah 55:8). We are also repeatedly reminded in the Scriptures that God's ways and man's ways have very different outcomes.

The Gospel of Luke sets God's ways in stark contrast to our own. In the first chapter we read Mary's song of praise, the Magnificat (Luke 1:46–55). She praises God for doing great things, for showing mercy, for scattering the proud and bringing down the powerful, for lifting up the lowly and feeding the hungry, for sending the rich away empty-handed. His selection of Mary—poor, young, powerless, and vulnerable—is itself a sign that his ways are intriguingly different.

The Lord is kind and merciful. He is slow to anger and rich in compassion (Exodus 34:6–7). But most people experience the world as cruel, harsh, mean, merciless, and uncompassionate. Why? God's ways are not man's ways, and all too often the ways of man rule the world. Jesus invites us to change that. He envisions a world that is lovingly directed by God's ways.

The Sermon on the Mount is the most famous speech ever given. In 141 words Jesus turns the world upside down and reminds us that God's ways are not ours.

> When Jesus saw the crowds, he went up the mountain; and after he sat down, his disciples came to him. Then he began to speak, and taught them, saying:
>
> "Blessed are the poor in spirit, for theirs is the kingdom of heaven.
>
> "Blessed are those who mourn, for they will be comforted.
>
> "Blessed are the meek, for they will inherit the earth.
>
> "Blessed are those who hunger and thirst for righteousness, for they will be filled.
>
> "Blessed are the merciful, for they will receive mercy.
>
> "Blessed are the pure in heart, for they will see God.
>
> "Blessed are the peacemakers, for they will be called children of God.
>
> "Blessed are those who are persecuted for righteousness' sake, for theirs is the kingdom of heaven.
>
> "Blessed are you when people revile you and persecute you and utter all kinds of evil against you falsely on my account. Rejoice and be glad, for your reward is great in heaven, for in the same way they persecuted the prophets who were before you. (Matthew 5:1-11)

In the epic parable of the prodigal son we see God's ways and man's ways richly contrasted. The younger son went off and squandered everything. The older son stayed at his father's side and attended to the family's interests (and his own). When the younger son returned broken, hungry, afraid, demoralized, and repentant, the father embraced him, forgave him, and rejoiced. The older brother did none of these things. He did not embrace his brother. He did not forgive his brother. He did not rejoice. Instead, he was full of judgment and self-pity (Luke 15). The older brother lived in a "self"-focused reality.

Forgiveness is at the center of God's heart, it is at the center of this story, and it is central to Christianity.

Left to our own devices, humans are vengeful. Even a cursory examination of human history will prove this beyond a doubt. Christianity proposes to change this, and the change is possible because of Jesus' radical example.

We are not naturally kind and merciful, slow to anger, and rich in compassion. These attitudes and behaviors are learned as we seek to walk in God's ways by living a life of virtue.

How should we respond to those who wrong us? This question is central to the life of every Christian. Nothing highlights the difference between God's ways and man's like forgiveness. Nothing highlights the difference between Christians and any other people on earth like forgiveness. And yet, this is just one example of how God's ways differ from our own.

The story of the prodigal son highlights another of the great differences between God and man. The father was abundantly generous. He said, "Quickly, bring out a robe—the best one—and put it on him; put a ring on his finger and sandals on his feet. And get the fatted calf . . . let us eat and celebrate" (Luke 15:22–23). The father's generosity was abundant and immediate. "Quickly" was his directive. Not "sometime tomorrow" or "in the next couple of weeks." But the older son was greedy, prideful, and selfish. He saw only what he was losing, not what he was gaining.

Are you a greedy person?

I have never met anyone who admitted to being greedy. I have encountered people who will confess to being gluttonous and prideful, and others who will say they have a problem with lust or anger, but I've never heard anyone admit greed. I've had deep and intimate conversations with thousands of people about the most personal aspects of their lives, but nobody has ever said to me, "I like money too much."

And nobody ever thinks of themselves as stingy. I have met some monumentally stingy people, but they think they are generous.

We don't see ourselves as we really are, and God's ways are not man's.

The other point that is essential to realize is that God's ways are not simply a minor adjustment of our own. They often represent the opposite end of the spectrum. Jesus invites us to a change in attitude, but that alone is not enough. Ultimately that change in attitude should lead to a change in behavior.

We opened this section with the verse from Isaiah, "Your thoughts are not my thoughts, nor are your ways my ways, declares the Lord." It is interesting that a connection is made here between thoughts and action. What we spend our days and weeks thinking about has an enormous impact on our actions.

What are you thinking? As you make your way to work each day, as you are waiting in the doctor's office or standing in the grocery store line, in those moments between activities, what do you think about?

I know this for certain: Whatever we spend these apparently inconsequential moments thinking about will increase in our lives. Few things will have more impact on your life than what you allow to occupy your mind. Use these times to ponder the ways of God and you will find yourself living them.

Ponder the Gospel and you will find yourself living it. This path is well trodden. For two thousand years, all those who have had any success in the Christian life, the great champions of Christianity, have had this in common: They all pondered the life and teachings set forth in the Gospels. Are you a Gospel thinker?

So much of our frustration in life is caused by rejecting the Gospel and trying to find a worldly solution to a spiritual problem. Every problem we experience has a spiritual dimension, but often we leave the spiritual dimension of things unconsidered.

The ways of God set out in the Gospels challenge our priorities. They remind us what matters most and what matters least. And make no mistake, it is not easy to walk in these ways. But the fruits of his ways are abundant. He will replace your confusion with clarity and wisdom, he will replace your anxiety with peace, and he will fill you with gratitude and joy even in the midst of great difficulty.

God is with us, even when we think he is not. God is in control, even when it appears that those who hate him are in control. And God is at work in our lives, even when it appears that everything is falling apart. God has a different way of doing things—a better way.

How we see other people and the world is at the core of the human experience. The Gospel equips us with a new lens. Through this lens we see other people, God, the world, and ourselves in a fundamentally different way than we did before. This is the Jesus effect. It changes our priorities, and by elevating them, it transforms the way we live and who we become.

Are you thriving or just surviving? If you're not thriving, why not? Perhaps it is time to abandon man's ways and embrace God's. Sometimes people ask, "How will I know when I am embracing

God's ways more?" It's a great question. Here is an easy litmus test: when you become less self-focused and more focused on others.

POINT TO PONDER: God has a better way of doing things.

VERSE TO LIVE: "The human mind may devise many plans, but it is the purpose of the Lord that will be established."
PROVERBS 19:21

QUESTION TO CONSIDER: What is one practical example of how God is inviting you to let go of *your* way and open yourself to *his* way?

PRAYER: Lord, teach me to value your way of doing things above all other ways.

THIRTY-TWO
The Real Problem

DON'T IGNORE THE REAL PROBLEM.

It is easy to lay Christianity out in a logical and reasonable way, and yet there are some questions that need to be addressed. Why in these two thousand years since Jesus walked the earth have so few people wholeheartedly embraced his teachings? Why do people like you and me, who want to follow his way more closely, struggle so monumentally and consistently to do so? What is the problem?

Paul wrote, "I do not do the good I want, but the evil I do not want is what I do" (Romans 7:19). This is the essential dilemma every Christian faces when we try to walk with God and live the teachings of Jesus Christ.

So, what is the real problem?

Watch the evening news and you will quickly come to the conclusion that the world is a bit of a mess. I don't know anyone who would say the world is moving in a great direction. As a parent of young children, I am concerned about the world they will inherit. Many grandparents try not to think about the world their grandchildren will experience because it makes them too anxious. They have seen enough of the change to recognize just how disturbing the trends are.

How did the world get to be a mess? Do you want the *truth* or some sugarcoated answer? Lots of people could give you lots of different reasons, answers, and excuses, but most of them would focus on only one aspect of the mess. They would talk about suffering and death, the collapse of the family, poverty and economic turmoil, or environmental breakdown. But these are all just symptoms. What's the disease?

If you get the flu, your symptoms may be a sore throat, a hacking cough, a fever, a runny nose, and aches and pains. But the only way to fix the symptoms is to cure the disease.

But let's get back to the question: How did the world get to be a mess? The big answer, the macro answer, is that people are sinful and they turn their backs on God.

Sin is the disease. Sin is the real problem. And the truth is, sin makes us unhappy.

God never intended for us to suffer and die. His original idea was for us to live in paradise forever. God's original plan was for ever-reigning peace between him, man, and the environment, and harmony between all men and women. Suffering and death are a direct result of sin.

Think about Gideon in the book of Judges. This whole book of the Bible is a series of stories that illustrate the Israelites' turning away from God and then turning back to him. Each time they embraced sin and turned away from God their lives became miserable. Each time they turned their backs on God they fell into another form of slavery. *Sin always leads to slavery of one kind or another*. But each time the Israelites turned back to God, they experienced peace and prosperity.

The same thing happens to us. When we turn away from God, our lives become miserable. Sure, there may be pleasure to be had in the moment, but the pleasure is fleeting, it's not sustainable, and after the pleasure of sin has faded there is just the misery it inevitably leaves behind. And every sin makes the world a little bit more of a mess.

Sin and evil are real. And they are not something that is "out there." They are in you and me. We each have the capacity for tremendous virtue and good, but we also have the capacity for sin and evil. These things are in us and we have to come to terms with them if we are going to live life to the fullest the way God wants us to.

So, what is sin? The Greek word for *sin* in the New Testament means "to miss the mark." If you were shooting an arrow at a target, this means that you would not only miss the bull's-eye, but you'd miss the whole target. Every sin, large or small, is in some measure a rejection of the-best-version-of-ourselves.

Sin is usually spoken about as a behavior that is wrong or immoral. And it is, but the only way to truly understand sin is in the context of the relationship between God and humanity. God is infinitely good and all his works are good. It is out of his goodness that he created us in his image and for good (Genesis 1:27–31).

Sin is more than just bad behavior. It is the rejection or destruction of something good. You cannot reject or destroy something that is good without rejecting *goodness itself.* God is goodness, and so every sin is in some way a rejection of God. This is why the most devastating dimension of sin is separation from God. Sin breaks down our relationship with him, puts obstacles between us and him.

We have a long history of turning away from God, offending him, and rejecting his goodness—this is where Jesus enters the story. The central claims of Christianity are that God became man in Jesus, that he died on the cross to atone for our sins, and that he rose from the dead to liberate us from death. But Jesus also came to show us the best way to live. Nobody can teach you more about the best way to live than Jesus.

Try this. Read the Gospel of Matthew. As you read about what Jesus taught, ask yourself, are these the solutions to the mess the world is in today? I think you will discover that Jesus has the antidote to the world's mess. Jesus is the solution.

What does this mean to you and me?

It is easy to say that the world is a mess. But the thing is, the more I become aware of who I really am, the more I discover that I'm a bit of a mess too. I do things every day that don't help me to become the-best-version-of-myself. And most of the time I don't actually want to do these things. Just like Paul wrote, "I do not do the good I want, but the evil I do not want is what I do" (Romans 7:19).

I am capable of incredible good, but sometimes I turn my back on God and his goodness. Sometimes I do it because I am stubborn and other times because I am lazy. Sometimes I turn my back on God and his goodness because the right path just seems too hard, and other times because I am selfish and just want what I want.

The truth is, I am a sinner, and sinners need a savior. The world is a mess and I am a mess, but Jesus came to fix the mess. That's good news.

The problem is sin. We don't like to talk about it, but that only leaves us tinkering with things that are inconsequential, trying hopelessly to make our lives better while ignoring the real problem. If we don't talk about sin—really talk about it and understand how it affects us and our lives—we cannot begin to solve the problems of our lives. Or the problems of the world. If we put sin aside, we find ourselves constantly dealing with the symptoms rather than addressing the disease.

What are the top ten problems in the world today? Make a list. We could argue about the order and maybe our lists would vary a little, but essentially we are likely to agree on the world's biggest problems. These are all just symptoms. Sin is the disease.

Science, politics, economics, and activism cannot solve the problem of sin.

What are the dominant problems in your own life? How are they connected to sin?

There is a cause-and-effect relationship between symptom and disease, between the problems of our lives and of the world and sin.

So, if sin is the problem, what is the solution? The answer isn't what, but who. Jesus is the solution.

It is impossible to speak honestly about Jesus without speaking about sin. That doesn't mean we have to start with it, but sooner or later, if we are really going to make any progress, the conversation must turn to sin—and not just in a sterile and academic way, but in a deeply personal way. Sin is deeply personal.

It is also impossible to make sense of Jesus without considering sin. It was sin that fractured humanity's relationship with God, and continues to. Jesus came to reconcile the human family to God. He accomplished this by dying for our sins. We brush over this idea because we are so familiar with it. But ask someone who has had a soul-crushing debt forgiven, and he will tell you about the overwhelming gratitude he felt (and continues to feel) for being given a second chance. The brutal death of Jesus on the cross is worthy of our deep reflection. The temptation is to look away, to walk away—just as we look away from our sin.

There are times when we feel that God is not with us. But in fact, the complete opposite is true. We are not with God. It isn't that God has abandoned us, but rather that we have abandoned God.

Have you wanted to put this book down during this section? We have a natural aversion to speaking of sin. It's normal. We have a tendency to run from our sin and hide from our shame. But what we are running from is nowhere near as important as what we are running toward. Let us run toward Jesus.

So, yes, the problem is sin. It is not a problem that is out there somewhere. It is not someone else's problem. It is my problem and your problem. It is something we must each decide to wrestle with. You can try to run from it like a coward, but sooner or later you will discover that it is an exercise in futility. You cannot run from yourself. You can confront this problem with all the courage you can muster, and wrestle with it with all your might, and still there will be days when it beats you down. On those days, pick yourself up, dust yourself off, and begin again.

POINT TO PONDER: Sin makes you unhappy.

VERSE TO LIVE: "Restore to me the joy of your salvation, and sustain in me a willing spirit." PSALM 51:12

QUESTION TO CONSIDER: What are your three most frequent sins?

PRAYER: Lord Jesus Christ, Son of God, have mercy on me and save me from my sins.

THIRTY-THREE
Comfortably Comfortable

ONE OF THE GREATEST TEMPTATIONS in life is to get comfortable.

Do you like being comfortable? Yeah, me too! If it's a little too hot or a little too cold when I get on a plane, I don't like that. If my favorite foods aren't easy to find, that irritates me. If the pillows in the hotel aren't just as I like them, it throws a ripple in my mood.

I like comfort—and there is so much comfort available. It is so easy to make comfort a priority in our lives. This leads to comfort addiction. Then even the slightest discomfort makes us irritable, restless, and discontent. Before long we are becoming one of those people who burst into an angry rage over the tiniest thing.

A couple of weeks ago, I was speaking with a friend, and he said something that really made me stop and reflect: "Everybody is looking for an easier, softer way." It's a generalization. It may not be true for *everyone*. But it sure seems true for most people. We want life to be easier. We want the path we walk to be softer. We want to be comfortable.

Is comfort good for us? Is the comfortable path the way of the Christian? It seems that it isn't. This is not simply my opinion. There are many things that may seem unclear when we read the Gospels, but the general criteria for following Jesus is abundantly clear. In Matthew's Gospel we read, "If anyone wishes to come after me, let him deny himself and take up his cross, and follow me" (Matthew 16:24). Deny yourself. Jesus was clear. He didn't promise or even allude to an easy path. He did not promise comfort. He promised quite the opposite. He set denial of self as a primary condition of discipleship, and he promised that each of us would have a cross of our own to carry.

Why doesn't Jesus want us to get comfortable? The reason is simple, profound, and practical: He doesn't want us to forget that we are just passing through this world. We are pilgrims. When we get comfortable we start to behave as if we are going to live on this earth forever—and we are not.

Perhaps if our lives have become comfortable that alone is a sign that we have wandered away from the Gospel path. When was the last time you denied yourself? Was it a large or small thing?

·•◆•·

One of the many aspects of the Gospel that fascinates me is how incredibly practical it is. Connected to this practicality of the Gospel is how it reaches into every facet of our lives. For example, there is a direct connection between a person's ability to succeed and his or her ability and willingness to delay gratification. How is this ability to delay gratification developed? By practicing the Gospel habit of denying ourselves.

Nothing will influence your success or failure at anything more than your ability (and willingness) to delay gratification. You cannot have a successful marriage without it, nor can your personal finances thrive. I cannot think of a noble career in which you can succeed without it, nor can you maintain a high level of physical health. You cannot successfully parent your children without it, and you cannot develop or maintain a vibrant spiritual life without it.

The ability to delay gratification, to deny yourself, is an essential life skill. So develop the habit of denying yourself in small ways a dozen times a day. Each time you deny yourself is a spiritual exercise, a spiritual push-up that strengthens the soul. This allows the soul to increasingly respond to grace and choose what is good, true, noble, and just in every situation.

Have a glass of water when you would rather have a Coke. Force yourself to work out when you would rather not. Take the long way home when you are impatient to get home. Have the fish when you are craving the steak. Wait five minutes before doing something you want to do right now.

There is something about denying ourselves that dissolves our blind spots and allows us to see things as they really are. The constant denial of self in small things gives us the clarity of heart, mind, and soul to see the present for what it really is and the future for what it still can be. This self-denial also allows us to see ourselves for who we really are, and to see in ourselves that best-version-of-ourselves that God created us to be. The daily denial of self allows us to see that we are sinful, but also opens us up to the grace we need in order to overcome our sinfulness.

Throughout the book, I have used the phrase "left to our own devices." What does that mean? It means to be without God's grace and the accountability of friendship and community. When we reject God's grace and the accountability of friendship and community, we become selfish. This selfishness manifests in a thousand different ways, but each of them is a turning on the self.

If you want to be a better Christian, start by denying yourself.

POINT TO PONDER: Being too comfortable, too often, makes us weak in mind, body, and spirit.

VERSE TO LIVE: "If anyone wishes to come after me, let him deny himself and take up his cross, and follow me."
MATTHEW 16:24

QUESTION TO CONSIDER: What is one way you can deny yourself today?

PRAYER: Jesus, thank you for all the comforts of this world; help me to discern when they are good for me and when they are not.

THIRTY-FOUR
Two Wrestling Questions

LIFE IS NOT ABOUT GETTING WHAT YOU WANT.

Questions play an important part in our lives. If you ask the wrong questions, you always get the wrong answers. It doesn't matter how much time you spend trying to work out the answer to the wrong question, and it doesn't matter how smart you are—the wrong questions never lead to the right answers.

What question are you preoccupied with at this time in your life? Is it the right question?

The world says that the preeminent question in your life is: What do you want? But life is not about getting what you want. At the same time, however, it is good, healthy, and important to *know* what you want.

Do you know what you want?

Do you spend time thinking about what you really want? If you're like most people, you don't have much time to spend thinking about anything. When was the last time you just took some time to go for a long walk or sit in a rocking chair and think about a single question? The most important things in life are almost never urgent. As a result, most people don't take the time to really think about life and don't truly know what they want.

You may say you want more money, a better job, to get married, to have a baby, to lose weight, a fabulous vacation . . . but what is behind or beneath all this wanting?

Motives can teach us so much about ourselves. By studying our motives we can grow exponentially in the spiritual life.

The thing about motives is that there is very rarely a single motive for anything.

Ask yourself why. Why do you want more money? So you can pay your bills. OK. Why else? So you won't feel anxious about running out of money. OK. Why else? So the people around you will respect you more. Is that healthy? Why else? So you can give your children a better life. Why else? So you don't have to work and be responsible and disciplined with money. OK. That could be a problem.

The thing about motives is that they are an entangled and unwinding web. We very rarely have a single motive for anything.

God gave us the ability to desire. To desire is human and God-given. It is healthy and good to explore our desires, for God often speaks to us through them. But the process is complicated by our disordered desires, which can be so many and scream so loud that we cannot hear God speaking to us through the deepest desires of our hearts.

Exploring what we really want will eventually lead us in the right direction if we have the discipline of reflection, unending persistence, and ever-increasing self-awareness. But it is a painfully slow path to where we all want to go.

There is another way. There is another question: What does God want?

As we rediscover Jesus and consider all that has happened in his name over the past two thousand years, one of the questions worthy of our pondering is: What does Jesus want? Take a moment. Think on that question. What do you think Jesus wants?

We find the answer to this question in chapter 15 of the Gospel of John. Jesus just finished describing himself as the vine, God the Father as the vine grower, and you and me as the branches. He then went on to say, "I have told you this so that my joy might be in you and your joy might be complete" (John 15:11).

He wants to share his joy with us. He wants your joy to be complete. He wants what you want. Beneath it all, at the depths of your being, what is it that you really want? You want complete joy. You want the kind of joy that only God can give you.

There are always two questions wrestling in our hearts: 1) What do I want? 2) What does God want? Over time we discover that what we really want, deep inside, is what God wants for us. Wisdom is the realization that it is insane to want something other than what God wants.

Once we realize this, we can begin the daily quest to seek his will in our lives.

POINT TO PONDER: The wrong questions always lead to the wrong answers.

VERSE TO LIVE: "May the God of hope fill you with all joy and peace." ROMANS 15:13

QUESTION TO CONSIDER: Does getting what you want bring you lasting happiness?

PRAYER: Jesus, please remind me when I forget that your will is what I really want deep down too.

THIRTY-FIVE

Complete Joy

ONLY GOD CAN GIVE YOU THE JOY YOU WANT.

You want a joy that is lasting and complete. This is a beautiful desire. You want lasting joy in a world where so few things seem to last. And you want a joy that is forever—not fleeting moments of pleasure, but a joy that goes on and on, with no end.

You want complete joy.

We may be confused about what will bring that complete joy. At different times in our lives we think that so many things, people, accomplishments, or pleasures will bring us the joy we desire, but they all leave us wanting.

The interesting thing is that God wants you to have complete joy. He created you for it. Jesus came so that you could be immersed in complete joy: "I have told you this so that my joy might be in you and your joy might be complete" (John 15:11).

Is your joy complete? If it isn't, why? What is diminishing your joy? Who or what is robbing you of joy? What's standing in the way of the complete joy that Jesus wants for you? How hard are you willing to work for that joy? What are you willing to sacrifice in order to have that complete joy? Are you getting in the way of your own joy?

And, perhaps *the* question in all of this: Does the Gospel offer the best path to this complete joy?

If you say, no, that's OK. I think you are wrong, but if you honestly feel that way, there is no shortcut. You have to explore why you feel that way. What is the alternate path that is better than the Gospel at leading people to the complete joy that we desire? Does it have a track record or is it just something you have imagined that allows you to do whatever you want under the false premise that someday, somewhere, somehow it will lead to complete joy?

The Gospel has a long track record of leading people to complete joy. I could list a thousand examples. But the beautiful thing is, you can test it for yourself and obtain instant proof.

Start to embrace the Gospel more—a little more, a lot more; that's up to you. But start to intentionally live the Gospel more each day. As you do, pay attention to the joy that increases in you. Pay attention to the clarity you have about what really matters and what doesn't. Pay attention to the stress and anxiety as it diminishes. Pay attention.

I think you want what Jesus wants. This is one of the classic discoveries of the spiritual journey. At some point as we grow in grace and awareness, we discover that we do indeed want what God wants for us: complete joy.

The Gospel is an invitation to and a blueprint for that complete joy.

POINT TO PONDER: Gratitude is a sure path to joy.

VERSE TO LIVE: "A joyful heart is life itself, and rejoicing lengthens one's life span." SIRACH 30:22

QUESTION TO CONSIDER: What really brings you joy?

PRAYER: Jesus, let me get out of the way so you can fill me with complete joy.

THIRTY-SIX
The Biggest Lie

THE LIES OF THIS WORLD suck the life out of us by destroying our joy.

A powerful case can be made for the Gospel. There is plenty of evidence that the joy we seek can be found by applying the teachings of Jesus to our lives. So, what is it that holds us back from fully embracing the Gospel of Jesus Christ?

Our fear and brokenness can be an obstacle. God invites us to a total surrender and we are afraid to let go. The culture and all its distractions can prevent us from seeing the beauty of the life God invites us to live. Self-loathing, unwillingness to forgive ourselves and others, biases and prejudices that have been born from past experiences, complacency toward others in need, selfishness—these are all real obstacles in our quest to authentically live the teachings of Jesus.

There are also the lies that are always swirling around Christianity. These lies can sow doubt in our hearts and minds, and erode our faith. There are so many lies in circulation about Christians and Christianity. Most are the result of ignorance. Some are the result of intentional misinformation. A handful are a malicious personal attack upon Jesus in an attempt to discredit the Christian faith. Some of these lies are aimed at our theology and beliefs, and others are aimed at the Christian way of life.

But one lie is having a diabolical impact on the lives of modern Christians. It is the biggest lie in the history of Christianity. It is worth noting that this lie is not one that non-Christians tell. It is a lie we tell ourselves as Christians.

This is the lie: Holiness is not possible.

The great majority of modern Christians don't actually believe that holiness is possible. Sure, we believe it is possible for our grandmothers or some medieval saint—just not for us. We don't actually believe that holiness is possible for us.

Search your heart. Do you believe holiness is possible for you?

I am not sure when or where this belief began its stranglehold on the spiritual life of Christians and the Church. No doubt there is a complex series of psychological reasons and excuses that cause us to accept and believe this lie. It is diabolical in its subtlety, evil genius in its simplicity.

It is astounding that just one lie can neutralize the majority of Christians. That's right, neutralize. This lie takes us out of the game and turns us into mere spectators in the epic story of Christianity. It may be the devil's biggest triumph in modern history. It is the holocaust of Christian spirituality.

In a thousand ways every day we tell ourselves and each other: Holiness is not possible. But it is a lie. And we cannot experience the complete joy that God wants for us and that we want for ourselves until we get beyond it.

POINT TO PONDER: You cannot get closer to God if you accept the lies of the world.

VERSE TO LIVE: "The righteous hate what is false."
PROVERBS 13:5

QUESTION TO CONSIDER: When did you stop believing holiness was possible for you?

PRAYER: Jesus, protect me from all the lies that seek to build a barrier between you and me, and remind me of my great destiny.

THIRTY-SEVEN
The Holy Moment

HOLINESS IS POSSIBLE.

The lie that has convinced so many Christians that holiness isn't possible is easy to disprove. It saddens me that we don't teach people how to overcome this debilitating lie. And the devastating truth is that it can be disproved in about ninety seconds. Let's take a look at it.

Suppose we are having coffee together and I say to you, "Can you go out tomorrow and create just one holy moment?" Not a holy day, or a holy hour, or even a holy fifteen minutes—just one holy moment.

You will probably ask, "What is a holy moment?"

A holy moment is a moment when you are being the person God created you to be, and you are doing what you feel God is calling you to do in that moment.

"I think I've got it," you say, "but tell me one more time—what is a holy moment?"

A holy moment is a moment when you are being the person God created you to be, and you are doing what you feel God is calling you to do in that moment.

"OK, I've got it," you confirm, and I ask again, "Can you go out tomorrow and create one holy moment?"

Sure you can. It's not overwhelming. It's not confusing. It doesn't require a massive intellect or a rare grasp of theology. It is accessible, achievable, and immensely practical. And here's the truly beautiful thing: It can be replicated. If you can do it once, you can do it twice. We don't need to have coffee again next week before you can create your second holy moment. You only need to learn the lesson of the holy moment once. From then on, you can apply it as many times as you decide to.

If you can create just one holy moment next Monday, you can create two on Tuesday and four on Wednesday, eight on Thursday, and so on. There is no limit to the number of holy moments you can create, other than your desire and the consciousness to grasp each moment for God as it is unfolding.

Now, it is important to note that you need God's grace to create holy moments. He will never deny you the grace you need. It is never God's grace that is lacking, but rather our willingness to cooperate with his grace.

Here are some examples of holy moments:

• Begin each day with a short prayer of gratitude, thanking God for giving you another day of life. This prayer can be short and simple. But turning to God in the first moment of the day is a great way to start and a fabulous way to set the stage for other holy moments throughout the day.

• Offer the least enjoyable tasks of your day to God as a prayer for someone who is suffering. This person's suffering could be physical, but suffering comes in an infinite number of disguises. You may know someone who is miserable at work, you may know someone who is struggling in his or her marriage, you may know someone who has an addiction. Offer your suffering for those people just as Jesus offered his suffering on the cross for us.

• Control your temper.

• Patiently coach someone who doesn't know how to do something or did something wrong.

• Go out of your way to do something for your spouse that you would rather not do, as an intentional act of love.

Opportunities to create holy moments are everywhere. In fact, every moment is an opportunity for holiness. Learning to grasp these opportunities one moment at a time is central to the Christian life.

Holiness is possible. This is the good news that Christians everywhere need to be convinced and reminded of. This is the good news that will raise us out of our neutralized, inactive state. This single beautiful truth transforms us into people of possibility. It opens up doors to live incredible lives, the incredible lives God created us to live. The truth that holiness is possible opens up our hearts, minds, and souls to new realities.

Among these new realities is the joy that comes from Gospel living. The lie that holiness is not possible keeps us from the joy that God wants us to experience. You don't need to work hard at creating holy moments for months or years before you start to experience this joy. The joy is immediate. Each holy moment brings with it an injection of joy.

Holiness is possible—for you! Try it, today! Remind yourself over and over again that it is possible. Say to yourself, "I can do that!"

POINT TO PONDER: Holiness is possible for you.

VERSE TO LIVE: "God's will is for you to be holy."
1 THESSALONIANS 4:3

QUESTION TO CONSIDER: Before now, did you ever believe holiness was possible for you?

PRAYER: Lord, never let me forget that holiness is possible.

THIRTY-EIGHT
What If?

HAVE YOU EVER CONSIDERED THE possibility that
it's *all* true?

The culture is constantly attacking Christianity, questioning
everything and casting doubts. Over time this constant under-
mining of the faith can begin to have a real effect on us. But what
if it all is true? What if everything Jesus talks about in the Gospels is true?

What if we really do need to account for the life we have lived?
What if heaven and hell do exist, the joy of eternity with God and
the eternal weeping of separation from him? Life, death, heaven,
hell, God, eternity, good and evil—what if it all is real?

Recently a friend shared a "What If?" letter that he had written and given to each of his children and their spouses at their
Thanksgiving dinner. He was gracious enough to allow me to include it here.

Dear Amy, Bruce, Emily, Katie, Ryan, and Andrew,

Have you ever stopped to wonder, "What if it's all true?" What do I mean by that? Well, I'm talking about everything that Jesus said, revealed, and fulfilled! We have heard it, listened to it, even from time to time have thought about it. Well, over the last year in particular I have been thinking about it a lot. It is a thought that will not leave me. I think that it is so "present in thought" to me because my Heavenly Father wants me to come to grips with it.

What does it really mean if it is ALL true? This much I know: If it is (and it is), then I can never be the same again. Not just one part of my life, not just an aspect here or there, but everything about me is forever to be changed. I can never be the same again.

Now, whoa, wait a minute—that is a pretty strong statement. That's right, it is. You see, I have come to understand that we have all spent our lives—at least those who even give God a moment in their thoughts and perhaps in their actions—hedging our bets. What do I mean by that? Well, we want to believe everything that Jesus says is true, but just to make sure, I am still going to make sure that I put myself first enough just to make sure I have a good time now and that I am going to be taken care of. I am not saying that we are not to be responsible for ourselves, particularly in providing for life's necessities. The last thing we are to do is be irresponsible. What I do mean is caring for me is not an end in itself but rather a launching pad to enable me to first and foremost care for those God has placed on the path before me.

If I spend my life preoccupied with me and my own happiness, I will live life missing the deepest joy that God has for me.

When you stop, when you come to understand and deeply believe that this is only the beginning of our eternal walk with God our Father, everything is different. Different instantly, different forever. You are overwhelmed with the beautiful, deep, joyful, and penetrating peace that comes from knowing that you are home today and forever. Fear is gone forever. You are like a ship that travels along a coast of endless safe harbors. Storms may come but the harbor is always moments away.

I use the analogy of a ship, because our new home with Christ, our new state of being, does not reside within four walls; on the contrary, it travels with us wherever we go. We have all been "dragged up from the deep" and have been set to sail into the wind, but from the safety of a ship that cannot be overcome by storm, famine, fear, anxiety, hunger, cold, loneliness, and despair. It is a ship ever on a new adventure but simultaneously anchoring in a safe harbor, being constantly provisioned.

You have but one Captain, your Father, who is the Creator and Lover of all. He is not "like" a Father; He is your Father. He is more truly your Father than I can ever be. This is a defining difference, which is the foundation of all that is true. Your faith in the saving grace of Christ is a game changer. Live in full son-ship and daughter-ship and receive the fullness of His love and constant care for you. He is your real Father every moment and beyond all time.

This new Captain under which you live and serve is like no other because He sends you forth in new freedom—a freedom that sets you free to do what you ought to do. To sail where you ought to sail. To explore and enjoy what you ought to explore and enjoy. It is your hands on the wheel but he is ever present and at your side as long as you invite Him to direct you. Draw courage, strength, and hope from Him. He is the farthest thing from a puppeteer. He is the truest friend any of us will ever know.

So, what if it is all true? How would that change the way you approach life today and in all your tomorrows? How would it impact the choices you make and the goals you pursue?

You are each at different junctures in your lives, as are your spouses, and your children. Where will your adventure take you and how will you go forth? Will you be like Peter, hedging your bet and looking at the storm-tossed waves? Or will you choose to see only the outstretched hand of Jesus? A hand that will never let you down. "What sort of man is this that even the winds and seas obey him?" (Matthew 8:27)

In the end it is a choice, an individual choice to be made every day and every hour. But it is always the same question: "Is it true, every bit of it?"

Make the decision.

Love,

Dad

•◦●◦•

I'd like to suggest two exercises. First, write a what-if letter to yourself. Second, write a what-if letter to someone in your life. You may decide to write to your children. You may decide to write to your parents. You may decide to write to an old college roommate, a friend from a job you used to have, or someone who crossed your path recently or long ago.

Some people will ignore such a letter. But for others it will be a life-altering moment.

•• ◆ ••

What if? It is a question worthy of our serious consideration.

And if it really is all as Jesus explains it, do you really want to be on the wrong side of it when your time comes?

We all die, and yet, so often we conduct our lives as if we were going to live forever. If you knew you were going to die one year from today, how would you change your life? Why are you waiting? Life is short. Too often we take for granted next week and next month and next year. We make plans for the future, not knowing if that future will be given to us. God gives us life one moment at a time, and he wants us to experience life in every breath we take.

God and life are always to be found in the now. Live each now passionately with God.

•• ◆ ••

God wants you to live your best possible life.

Forget about yesterday. Forget about all your yesterdays. You cannot change them. God is more interested in your future than he is in your past—but he is most interested in your now! Starting right now, today, God wants you to begin intentionally living your best life.

How is the best way to live? This is the question that the great thinkers of every age grapple with. It is also a question that we each wrestle with in a deeply personal way. We are all searching for the best way to live. Sometimes it is a conscious search and sometimes it is an unconscious yearning for something more or different.

The best way to live is one of life's biggest questions. It is a question we must each answer for ourselves. I have come to the conclusion that the radical Gospel of Jesus Christ is the best way to live. I have thought long and hard about this, explored dozens of alternative philosophies, and foolishly tried to come up with my own self-interested way of living, but all of these fell short.

I am totally convinced that the life Jesus invites us to in the Gospels is the best way to live. In fact, I am so convinced that even if you could prove to me that God does not exist, that eternity does not exist, and that after we die we simply cease to exist, I would still believe that the teachings of Jesus offer the best way to live.

I am a practical man. The Gospel works. It helps everyone who embraces it to increasingly become more perfectly themselves. It celebrates the dignity of the human person, which is a primary truth that is indispensable if we are to understand the world around us. It fosters phenomenal relationships and encourages vibrant and orderly community. It promotes right relationships between humanity and nature. It just works. In an amazingly practical way, the Gospel is the answer to all the deeply personal questions of life and the light that shows us the next step to take in our journey. There is simply no better way to live.

Some days I am woefully inadequate in my attempts to live this Gospel. Sometimes this is because I am sinful and selfish and weak and broken. Other times it is because I am proud, stubborn, resistant, arrogant, and attached to my own ways. So, no, I don't always live up to the life-giving invitation God extends to me in the Gospel. But I know this: I am always happier when I am trying to. I have observed myself enough to know that there is a direct connection between my effort to live the Gospel and the amount of joy in my soul.

I don't know of a better way to live. Do you? The Gospel is pure genius. It is the ultimate worldview, the most complete spiritual manual, and the best way to live.

Isn't it time you gave yourself over wholeheartedly to the pursuit of a Gospel life?

POINT TO PONDER: The chances of it all being true are very high.

VERSE TO LIVE: "Teach me to do your will, for you are my God. Let your good spirit lead me on a level path." PSALM 143:10

QUESTION TO CONSIDER: If you were dying, would you be paying more attention to your spiritual health than you are today?

PRAYER: Jesus, guide my words, thoughts, and actions so that I can live my best life and become the-best-version-of-myself.

THIRTY-NINE
People of Possibility

GOD WANTS TO FILL YOU WITH HOPE so you can
see the possibilities.

There is one type of person everyone loves having on their
team at work: the person who makes things happen. Ask her to
take care of something and you never have to think about it again;
you don't have to wonder whether she took care of it. Give her a
problem and she jumps in and gets it solved. Ask her to do something really difficult that she has never done before and she re-
plies, "No problem. We will find a way to get it done." These are
people of possibility.

Christians should be the ultimate people of possibility. But too
often we are people of impossibility. Suggest that something new
or different be done in your community and often all you will hear
are reasons why it can't be done. "We don't have enough money."
"Too many other things going on." "It won't work." "People won't
come." "We've tried something like that before."

Our churches should be palaces of possibility. Christians more
than anyone else should be a people of possibility. But too often

we are negative, with our gaze cast downward and backward, lacking joy and behaving like people of impossibility.

Would the Holy Spirit ever bear this pessimism? Pessimism belongs to the slaves of this world, not to the children of God.

This kind of pessimism has a twin brother: cynicism. Both are enemies of faith. We live in a cynical time. Cynicism strangles joy, kills hope, and fills our hearts and minds with doubt.

These are trying times for people of faith. But when my heart is weary and my mind is tortured, I always return to two truths. The first is this: Christianity has never failed. It is simply incapable of failure. Many have failed to live the Christianity they professed, but that is human failure, not the failure of Christianity. Whenever and wherever the teachings of Jesus have been taken seriously, the results have been astounding, and yet remarkably similar.

Throughout history, over and over again, when someone has wholeheartedly embraced Jesus and his teachings, that person has been transformed from a shadow of his real self into a shining example of what the human person is actually capable of when we allow God to direct our lives. Men and women of all faiths who cross paths with that person have been lovingly challenged to reconsider their own lives. Many have been won to new and exciting relationships with God through that person's example. They in turn spread compassion, joy, and wisdom to others who cross their path. Every man and woman who embraces the teachings of Jesus sets off an astounding domino effect of love of God and neighbor.

Christianity works.

The second truth that I direct my heart and mind to in times of discouragement is this: If Christians behaved like Christians, the world would be a very different place. There are two billion Christians on the planet today. How would the world be different if we Christians simply behaved as Christians? Imagine.

It is time to refocus on the essential invitation of Christianity that is found in the Gospels. It is an invitation to complete joy delivered by Jesus Christ.

It is time to rediscover Jesus.

POINT TO PONDER: Open your heart, mind, and soul to the possibilities.

VERSE TO LIVE: "For God all things are possible."
MATTHEW 19:26

QUESTION TO CONSIDER: Have you ever tried to live Christianity wholeheartedly?

PRAYER: Lord, help me to see the possibilities.

FORTY

An Hour of Power

YOU CAN LEARN MORE IN AN HOUR of silence than you can in a year from books.

There are so many moving passages that we read throughout the Gospels about Jesus' life—moments of monumental victory and moments of desperate disappointment. And yet, some of the most touching moments for me are when Jesus unabashedly displayed his humanity.

We witness one of these moments on the last night of Jesus' life. He was in the garden of Gethsemane praying and he asked the disciples to watch with him. He went a short distance away to pray, and when he returned, they were asleep. "Could you not stay awake with me one hour?" Jesus said to them (Matthew 26:40).

Jesus didn't want to be alone. How very human. He wanted company. The humanity of Jesus is a beautiful thing. I wish we got more glimpses into his humanity through the Gospels. I'd love to know what his sense of humor was like. I'd love to know what he hoped and feared. Jesus' divinity is awesome, but his humanity is just as awesome.

I love churches that are full, bursting at the seams, filled with energy and enthusiasm. I love seeing a community raise the roof with fabulous music. I love seeing the grounds of a church that is buzzing with activity, people moving this way and that to attend some type of ministry or just to spend some time in fellowship.

But I also love an empty church. I love sitting there, with nobody but God and me. There is something powerful about that.

So many of us are afraid of silence and petrified by solitude, but we need some silence and solitude to sit with God and work out who we are, what we are here for, what matters most, and what matters least, so that we can make great decisions in our lives. We need that.

This is my final challenge to you: Sometime in the next few days, find an empty church and sit with Jesus for an hour. Don't place great plans or expectations on that hour. Just sit with him, for a full hour. Just be with him in the silence.

It may be uncomfortable at first. That's natural. You will want to leave after a few minutes. That's natural too, because we live in a world that says we always need to be active. But being with God—prayer—is like atomic energy: a contraction that produces an expansion. We draw back from the world (contraction) so that we can live more fully in the world (expansion).

God doesn't want you to live in your past and he certainly doesn't want you living in your fears. God wants you to live in his power now.

Say with me:

"I am the son/daughter of a great king. He is my father and my God. The world may praise me or criticize me. It matters not. He is with me, always at my side, guiding and protecting me. I do not fear because I am his."

Say it loud. Say it proud. Post it on your wall somewhere, and pause to be reminded each day.

God wants you to live in his power. The only question is: How?

People don't do anything until they get inspired. But once they are inspired there is almost nothing they can't do. I often think about the disciples hiding in the upper room, scared to death, operating from a place of fear. But then the Holy Spirit comes, and boom! They are suddenly ready to go out and change the world. How? They got inspired. I mean, it was a lot more than that, and it was the ultimate form of inspiration, but inspiration was the difference.

Inspiration is the difference. Lots of people are knowledgeable, but some move men's and women's hearts, stir their souls, and inspire them to take action.

Get inspired. What inspires you? What can you do each day, each week, and each month that will keep you inspired to live in God's power? It may be time in a quiet, empty church; it may be singing in the church choir; it may be reading great books. Whatever it is, find it and cling to it. People need inspiration for their souls like they need water for their bodies.

Allow God to inspire you, to fill you with his power, because he wants to send you out to inspire others.

Who are you going to inspire today?

I hope you have enjoyed

Rediscover Jesus

It has been a great privilege to write for you.
May God bless you with a prayerful spirit
and a peaceful heart.

Matthew Kelly

ALSO BY MATTHEW KELLY

ABOUT THE AUTHOR

MATTHEW KELLY has dedicated his life to helping people and organizations become the-best-version-of-themselves! Born in Sydney, Australia, he began speaking and writing in his late teens while he was attending business school. Since that time, four million people have attended his seminars and presentations in more than fifty countries.

Today Kelly is an internationally acclaimed speaker, author, and business consultant. His books have been published in more than twenty-five languages, have appeared on the *New York Times*, *Wall Street Journal*, and *USA Today* bestseller lists, and have sold more than fifteen million copies.

He is also the founder of The Dynamic Catholic Institute, a Cincinnati based non-profit organization whose mission is to re-energize the Catholic Church in America by developing world-class resources that inspire people to rediscover the genius of Catholicism.

Kelly is also a partner at Floyd Consulting, a Chicago based management-consulting firm.

His personal interests include golf, piano, literature, spirituality, and spending time with his wife Meggie and their children Walter, Isabel, Harry, and Ralph.